ENGAGING IN THE
SCHOLARSHIP OF
TEACHING
AND
LEARNING

ENGAGING IN THE SCHOLARSHIP OF TEACHING AND LEARNING

A Guide to the Process, and How to Develop a Project From Start to Finish

Cathy Bishop-Clark
and
Beth Dietz-Uhler

Foreword by Craig E. Nelson

STERLING, VIRGINIA

COPYRIGHT © 2012 BY STYLUS PUBLISHING, LLC.

Published by Stylus Publishing, LLC
22883 Quicksilver Drive
Sterling, Virginia 20166-2102

Library of Congress Cataloging-in-Publication Data

Bishop-Clark, Cathy, 1964–
    Engaging in the scholarship of teaching and learning : a guide to the process, and how to develop a project from start to finish / Cathy Bishop-Clark and Beth Dietz-Uhler. — First edition.
        pages   cm
    Includes bibliographical references and index.
    ISBN 978-1-57922-470-7 (cloth : alk. paper) — ISBN 978-1-57922-471-4 (pbk. : alk. paper) — ISBN 978-1-57922-811-8 (library networkable e-edition) — ISBN 978-1-57922-812-5 (consumer e-edition)   1. Education—Research.   2. Learning—Research.   3. College teaching—United States.   I. Dietz-Uhler, Beth.   II. Title.
    LB1028.B4766   2012
    370.72—dc23
                                                                                    2012002073

13-digit ISBN: 978-1-57922-470-7 (cloth)
13-digit ISBN: 978-1-57922-471-4 (paper)
13-digit ISBN: 978-1-57922-811-8 (library networkable e-edition)
13-digit ISBN: 978-1-57922-812-5 (consumer e-edition)

Printed in the United States of America
All first editions printed on acid free paper that meets the
American National Standards Institute Z39-48 Standard.

Bulk Purchases
Quantity discounts are available for
use in workshops and for staff development.
Call 1-800-232-0223

First Edition, 2012

10 9 8 7 6

I dedicate this book to my mother—the person who never allowed me to think "I can't" and who has always been my biggest fan. Thank you, Mom—for everything.

—Cathy Bishop-Clark

I dedicate this book to all of my former students for inspiring me to want to become a better teacher.

—Beth Dietz-Uhler

Contents

Acknowledgments

WE WOULD like to acknowledge and thank the members of our Scholarship of Teaching and Learning Faculty Learning Communities. The feedback we received from them inspired this book. They helped us to understand what needed additional clarification and explanation, helped expand our own understanding of SoTL, and most importantly shared our enthusiasm about the field.

We particularly want to thank those who took the time to write quotes that we included in this book: Michelle Abraham, Assistant Professor of Psychology; Debbie Beyer, Associate Professor of Nursing; Mary Jane Brown, Visiting Instructor of English, Alan Cady, Professor of Zoology; Donna Evans, Instructor of Computer Science and Academic Advising; Kelli Johnson, Associate Professor of English; Eric Luczaj, Associate Professor of Computer Science; Gina Petonito, Visiting Assistant Professor of Sociology and Gerontology; Eva Rodriguez Gonzalez, Assistant Professor of Spanish and Portuguese; and Jennifer Yamashiro, Lecturer of Art and Interim Director of the Honors Program.

While all of the members of our learning communities created successful SoTL projects, we have chosen to highlight Brooke Flinders's project. Brooke came to the community with a few vague, broad ideas. She simplified her ideas, organized a pilot study, and followed up with a full-blown study. Shortly after the learning community ended, she secured a $2 million grant for a five-year project related to her SoTL work. We thank Brooke for writing the closing comments of the book and sharing her experiences.

Kathleen McKinney deserves a special thank you for spending time with us at the very beginning stages of this effort. She unselfishly shared her resources, talent, and time. We appreciate the work of our editor John von Knorring whose comments improved the content in many ways. Thank you to Tammy Lewis for her administrative support throughout the project, and to Amy Stander for her excellent editing.

Foreword

THE SCHOLARSHIP of Teaching and Learning (SoTL) has become a major force for transforming higher education. The initial development and rapid spread of SoTL were fostered largely by the Carnegie Foundation for the Advancement of Teaching and the American Association for Higher Education through their sponsorship of the activities of the Carnegie Academy for the Scholarship of Teaching and Learning and related groups. At its core, SoTL invites faculty to take learning seriously by better defining what outcomes are most important for the students to master and then assessing the extent to which their current learning designs have led to such mastery (Biggs & Tang, 2007). Note that this shifts the focus away from the quality of students to the effectiveness of the learning design (Brabrand, 2006). This change allows us to redesign our courses and programs to increase achievement, retention, and equity. And the focus on outcomes will help us develop students who are better critical thinkers, more effective communicators, and further advanced in their professional ethics and in life skills (Association of American Colleges and Universities, 2010; Baxter Magolda, 2009; Biggs & Tang, 2007). The change also will allow us to empower our graduates to more effectively think about complex issues including economic disparity, international conundrums, and science and society policy issues including changes in health care, climate change, and genetically modified crops.

Given its deep importance, it is not surprising that much recent scholarship has focused on SoTL. A recent Amazon search returned 1,237 suggestions. I examined the first 160 briefly. Of these, 94 actually seemed be about SoTL in some important way: 53 focused on applications of SoTL, an additional 35 had SoTL as the major focus of the book, and only six were guides to doing SoTL.

Bishop-Clark and Dietz-Uhler have made a unique contribution in the present volume. It is an exception-ally fine, straightforward, and brief guide for faculty looking at their first SoTL project. For most such readers, it will probably seem to be the most helpful of the guides. The others often will seem more helpful after the first project has been completed. The core of this book is essentially an individualized workshop—complete with resources, detailed examples, and both example and blank worksheets. The workshop chapters are clearly based on the authors' experience in guiding face-to-face group workshops. They lead sequentially from selecting and refining a research idea through designing the study and collecting and analyzing the data and to considering alternative methods and sites for presenting and publishing the results. At each stage, careful consideration is given to alternative approaches and to ways of making better choices. The workshop chapters are preceded by two chapters of introduction and are followed by a concluding chapter on challenges and solutions—one that includes a careful consideration of ways of helping the academy give more importance to SoTL. The appendices provide good lists of conferences and journals that are appropriate for presenting SoTL results. And, although it is written with the novice in mind, many of us with more experience also will benefit from reading through it.

As you will see, the text is unusually engaging. Each chapter includes a nice mix of examples drawn from the authors' work and those taken from the literature. Introductory and summary statements are used generously making it very easy to keep track of what they are asking you to do and to think about. I especially liked the opening and closing stories and the repeated use of points drawn from the authors' personal histories. Many helpful citations are integrated throughout—I found several that I followed up on immediately.

I anticipate that this book will lead many more faculty members to see their teaching as an opportunity to engage in SoTL. And, even though it is clearly an effective guide for individual thinking, it will be even more effective when used as the focus of a Faculty Learning Community or by a less formal group of faculty working together. Indeed, the core structure and especially the worksheets will help groups to stay focused and productive. However used, it will help teachers use SoTL as a way to improve their students' learning and to foster more advanced learning outcomes while simultaneously enhancing the faculty members' own professional development and careers. I hope you find it as interesting and helpful as I did.

CRAIG E. NELSON
Emeritus Professor of Biology, Indiana University,
and Founding President, International Society
for the Scholarship of Teaching and Learning

References

Association of American Colleges and Universities. (2010). *VALUE: Valid assessment of learning in undergraduate education.* Retrieved from http://www.aacu.org/value/metarubrics.cfm

Baxter Magolda, M. B. (2009). *Authoring your life: Developing an internal voice to navigate life's challenges.* Sterling, VA: Stylus.

Biggs, J., & Tang, C. (2007). *Teaching for quality learning at university* (3rd edition). Open University Press: UK

Brabrand, C. (2007). *Teaching-teaching & understanding-understanding. Daimi Edutainment.* Distributed by Aarhus University Press. Retrieved from: http://www.daimi.au.dk/~brabrand/short-film/ and http://video.google.com/videoplay?docid=-5629273206953884671).

Introduction to the Scholarship of Teaching and Learning

WELCOME TO THE exciting world of the Scholarship of Teaching and Learning (SoTL). SoTL is the study of teaching and learning and the communication of findings so that a body of knowledge can be established. This book focuses on the scholarly tools and innate curiosity about teaching and learning that you already possess and seeks to help you develop these tools so that you approach scholarly curiosity in the classroom in a more formal manner. This formalization strengthens the scholarly credibility of your findings, which facilitates your sharing this work to contribute to the body of knowledge on SoTL. The book is based on a five-step process that helps you take that sometimes vague curiosity and turn it into a publishable SoTL project.

In this first chapter, we discuss the benefits and rewards of engaging in SoTL as well as the need for SoTL. We spend some time reviewing the standards of SoTL so that we have a sense of how rigorous this work must be. Next, we briefly review the steps of doing SoTL and how the book can help you complete a SoTL project from start to finish. Finally, we discuss the role of students in SoTL, a topic that we highlight in each subsequent chapter.

We begin this book by sharing our individual stories. We describe our SoTL journey, why we started SoTL work, and where it has taken us. The first story, Beth Dietz-Uhler's, describes how she started as a disciplinary-only researcher and later found herself deeply immersed in SoTL. The second story, Cathy Bishop-Clark's, describes how SoTL has influenced her teaching, her service, and her research. We hope that each story illustrates that SoTL has motivated us to become better teachers who are able to facilitate student learning more effectively, has contributed to the body of literature that helps educators better understand teaching and learning, and has helped create rewarding and incredibly interesting careers.

Beth Dietz-Uhler's Story

I am a social psychologist with disciplinary research interests in small-group behavior, computer-supported interaction, and the psychology of sport fans and spectators. I earned my PhD at a research university. I began my career on the "main" campus at Miami University in a department that highly valued disciplinary research. Although I valued teaching deeply, my primary scholarly interests were in social science research. At the time, I paid little attention to how I could approach my teaching in a scholarly fashion or even how my classroom could be a source of scholarly interest. I was a successful researcher and teacher.

Four years after beginning work as a visiting assistant professor on the main campus, I applied for and obtained a tenure-track position on one of the university's regional campuses. My teaching load increased from two courses per semester to four. Because the regional campus is open enrollment, the types of students in my classes were quite different from those on the main campus. I found myself instantly intrigued by the diversity of students and how I could design learning opportunities that would appeal to *all* of the students in my classes. I started reading books about teaching and learning, and I started attending conferences on teaching and learning. Most important, I began thinking deeply about teaching and learning, wondering how I could improve my teaching and have an impact on students' learning.

My interest in SoTL was aided by my new colleagues on the campus who valued approaching teaching and learning from a scholarly perspective. Most influential was my association with Cathy Bishop-Clark. Although we came from different disciplines, we found that our teaching philosophies and styles were quite similar. She began to share with me her interests in SoTL and showed me how her teaching, service, and research were all intricately connected. We started to talk about ideas for teaching and learning projects in our classes that would produce data and allow us to determine whether the projects successfully improved learning. Our first SoTL project together, which was published 10 years ago, was based on an observation I had in one of my classes. After sharing the observation with Cathy, we decided to run an experiment to test our hunches about it. That experiment was instrumental in solidifying my interests in SoTL.

From that point on, I began to think about teaching and learning from a scholarly perspective. I started to think of my classroom as a research laboratory where I could ask questions about students' learning and collect information to find answers. I also started immersing myself in the SoTL literature. These new ways of thinking, as well as an awareness of the SoTL literature, gave me new ideas about teaching, learning, and SoTL projects. I started presenting and publishing the results of my SoTL projects, many of which I conducted with colleagues not even in my discipline. In short, I was hooked on SoTL!

While I did not entirely abandon my scholarship in my discipline, my production of disciplinary research did decrease. When I stood for promotion to associate professor and tenure, I had a solid record of teaching, service, and research. At the time, I had published 16 peer-reviewed articles in my discipline and one peer-reviewed SoTL article, so I did not need to worry that my increased engagement in SoTL and decreased pro-

ductivity in disciplinary research would hinder my chances of being promoted and tenured. But when I stood for promotion to professor five years later, I was a little nervous because I had almost as many SoTL publications (seven) as I did disciplinary ones (nine) since being tenured and promoted to associate professor. Because my institution does value SoTL, I was promoted to professor.

Since being promoted to professor, my scholarship focuses almost exclusively on SoTL, not because of a lack of interest in my discipline, but because I find myself more and more excited about SoTL. Why does SoTL excite me so much? Because I get revved up when I think about SoTL projects. I get excited by the possibility of trying something new in the classroom and collecting information to determine whether my idea was successful and if it positively affected students' learning. I get excited about answering questions about teaching and learning from the same scientific approach that I answer disciplinary questions. I get excited by SoTL because I want my students to have valuable and rewarding learning opportunities.

Cathy Bishop-Clark's Story

As Beth's story illustrates, we work at an institution that places tremendous value on teaching and learning. Because of this, my primary form of scholarship throughout my career has been in SoTL. All of my promotions: associate, full, and administration, have been partially based on a record that consists largely of SoTL work. In 2008 I received a prestigious teaching award at the university, and my SoTL work was the primary reason. SoTL has energized my teaching, helped keep my knowledge current, and influenced my department's directions in multiple ways over the years. Over the course of 20 years, I have published approximately 25 papers related to SoTL studies and presented about 50 times in teaching and learning conferences.

In the beginning of my career, I started researching teaching and learning issues for two reasons. First, I was incredibly interested in what was happening in my classroom. I spent the majority of my time working with students and helping them to understand the fundamentals of computer science. I wanted to better understand how they were learning and whether I could do anything to improve their learning. I wanted to see them entering the next course with a firm understanding of content, an improved ability to solve problems, and a positive attitude about their future courses. More often than not, students left the course with a limited understanding of fundamental concepts, and many students left the courses I taught for nonmajors never wanting to take another computing course. The second reason I moved into SoTL work was practical. My teaching load on a regional campus was 12 credit hours each semester, and that left little time for anything else. For me personally, to maintain a reasonable workload and manage my time effectively, I needed to integrate teaching, scholarship, and service. To achieve significant accomplishments in teaching and research, SoTL research was a very attractive alternative to disciplinary research.

For the first phase of my career (pretenure and assistant professor), I studied students in my courses and in my colleagues' computer science courses. Virtually all of these students were categorized as novice students. I investigated whether the use of some of the newest programming languages helped students to understand fundamental concepts in a deeper and more substantial way. The outcomes of those studies resulted in the department's changing the programming language used for its first computer science course.

In the associate professor phase of my career, I became interested in investigating teaching and learning issues with colleagues outside my own discipline. Because I worked on a campus with many nontraditional students, I worked with a sociologist to study the differences in attitude, perceptions, and learning between traditional and nontraditional students. Additionally, Beth Dietz-Uhler and I team-taught a course on the psychology of the Internet. Most class sessions were not only sessions on the topic, but were also research studies. We studied our students as they learned and ourselves as we taught. I found it both interesting and enlightening to study teaching and learning with my sociology and psychology colleagues.

In the professor phase of my SoTL career, I became interested in helping others find the type of satisfaction and energy that SoTL provided me. With Beth, I facilitated several learning communities where we led groups of faculty through their own first SoTL projects. At the same time, I moved into administration. The grounding I achieved through my SoTL work has provided a foundation for the way I work as an administrator. My studies on teaching and learning included careful, systematic, and data-driven investigations. This kind of process continues to inform my work as an administrator.

Why We Wrote This Book

Both of us have been engaged in SoTL for more than a dozen years. We are both passionate about our work in the classroom, and we are also passionate scholars. As such, we approach our teaching from a scholarly perspective, always asking why this worked or why that didn't or how we can improve our teaching and enhance our students' learning. We have spent many years engaging with and being engaged by our colleagues on our observations in the classroom. Several years ago, we were asked to do a 90-minute workshop on the scholarship of teaching and learning. We jumped at the opportunity. We were also overly ambitious, thinking we could help participants work through the steps of a SoTL project in 90 minutes! Since then, we have conducted numerous workshops (some more scaled-down and some that involved a half-day) and faculty learning communities on how to do SoTL.

When we started doing workshops, participants encouraged us to start faculty learning communities as well so we could guide participants through all of the stages of their individual SoTL projects. It was in those faculty learning communities that we began to develop worksheets that provided prompts for participants to think about as they worked through all of the steps of their SoTL projects. The worksheets in this book are nearly identical to the ones we've used in our faculty learning communities. We realized, when modifying these worksheets for this book, that we would not be present to provide the feedback we provide to our workshop and faculty learning community participants, so we tried to write with enough detail to provide much of this feedback on the worksheets.

Engaging in SoTL has made me more aware of simple ways I can assess the effectiveness of my teaching. I don't need to engage in full-scale studies in order to design classroom activities to include clear goals and means of assessing students' progress toward them. Simply having designed and completed a single SoTL study has brought more precision into my everyday teaching. —MARY JANE, ENGLISH

We suspect that you are already an excited scholar of teaching and learning. We hope sharing our enthusiasm for SoTL might spark new questions and new ideas about your teaching and your students' learning. We hope you will work through all of the steps of SoTL and complete a SoTL project that we will learn about when you share your results in future conferences and journals!

Introduction to SoTL

As we mentioned, we spend a good deal of time thinking about what goes on in the classroom. When we try a new activity that goes well, or have a class discussion that really seems to engage students, or listen to a student presentation that suggests that students learned what we intended, we get excited! We sometimes get so excited that we rush back to our offices to tell or e-mail our colleagues. Sometimes we even call our families to tell them.

Despite all of this excitement, we still have questions. Why did this activity seem so successful? How do I really know students learned? What information do I need to have to really be sure that the activity improved student learning? What information will I need to convince my colleagues that this new activity improved student learning?

We've also had something like this happen: We try a new activity based on a new idea we've had or one of our colleagues had or even one found in a journal that sounded relevant to our class. We are excited that the new activity will engage students in a deeper way and enhance their learning of a particular concept. The activity bombs! Students are not engaged; they complain they do not like the activity. Exam scores on the concept suggest that students did not learn the concept at a level we intended. We feel a sense of frustration, but the experience also piques our curiosity: Why did this activity not work in the way we intended?

Whether our teaching strategies are successful or unsuccessful, we are always asking ourselves these questions:

- Why did this teaching strategy (activity, lecture, discussion, etc.) work or not work?
- Why did it or did it not achieve the intended outcome(s)?
- What information (e.g., exam scores, student writing) will I need to determine whether the teaching strategy achieved the intended outcome(s)?
- Once I have the information, how can I use it to determine whether the teaching strategy was effective?
- How, when, and with whom will I share my experiences?

We routinely ponder these questions on an informal, sometimes subconscious level. We are constantly curious about our teaching and our students' learning because we want to be better teachers. If you are reading this book, then it is likely that you are also motivated to be a better teacher. In fact, it is likely that you ask yourself these same questions all the time. If you do, then you are already a scholar of teaching and learning—perhaps not in the formal sense, but in spirit.

Benefits of SoTL

As you can imagine, there are multiple benefits of engaging in SoTL activity. For us, SoTL has provided many positive outcomes, including making us more-informed teachers, allowing us to collaborate with other colleagues in different disciplines, and improving our students' learning. Chism (2008) suggests that SoTL has three main benefits. First, engaging in SoTL improves student learning because it affects how faculty members think about teaching and learning opportunities for their students. Second, contributions to the field of teaching are improved and enhanced. Third, engaging in SoTL enriches one's experiences as a teacher. Similarly, Weimer (2006) lists several reasons why SoTL improves one's teaching. These include:

- Allows for the exploration of questions that interest you
- Helps you to develop instructional awareness
- Encourages you to think more deeply about teaching and learning
- Improves teaching for the right reasons
- Keeps your teaching fresh over the long haul

- Improves conversations with colleagues
- Fosters learning in new ways and from new people

In a study on community college scholarship, Kelly-Kleese (2003) found that the predominant reasons faculty engaged in scholarship "had to do with a sense of self-fulfillment, personal interest, and commitment to being the best instructors they can be, improving their teaching, their programs, and the college as a whole" (p. 79). Nelson (2003) describes three reasons why teaching is likely to be excellent if informed by SoTL. First, when teachers are informed by SoTL, they will have a more powerful framework with which to think about their own teaching and their students' learning. Second, teachers informed by SoTL are likely to start questioning their assumptions about poor performance in their classes. Third, being informed by SoTL provides more examples and ideas to try in one's own classroom.

Conducting research about teaching practices informs the learner (the student) and it enhances my teaching and my understanding of how students learn. I cannot think about a better example where research and teaching go together.
—EVA, SPANISH

Without a doubt, engaging in SoTL is good for our teaching and our students' learning. For us, SoTL causes us to be more attuned to what happens in the classroom—we spend more time thinking through a teaching strategy, we become more connected to our students, and we think more about the evidence we need to convince others that students learned what we intended. We also enjoy our teaching more when we think of it as a scholarly activity.

The Need for SoTL

It is probably clear by now that reflecting on your teaching and students' learning improves teaching and learning. So why not just leave it at that? Why not just be comfortable spending time thinking about what goes on in the classroom, making changes and alterations to improve what we do, and improving student

learning? Several reasons to conduct more formal SoTL activities come to mind.

First, without empirical evidence, we cannot be sure that anything we do in the classroom is effective (Grauerholz & Zipp, 2008). Sure, we have exam scores and student papers and presentations to which we assign grades, so we know how students are performing in our classes. But do we know that students are really learning what we intend for them to learn? We have a pretty good idea and probably quite a bit of confidence that most of our students are attaining learning outcomes. But our hunches and anecdotal evidence are not going to convince many people. In our disciplinary research, we would not say, for example, "Based on my experiences, it seems as though people are more likely to help another person when fewer people are around than when there are many people." Instead, we would provide empirical evidence based on, in this case, a scientific study, to show that people are more likely to help in less-crowded situations than they are in more-crowded situations. To be convincing that a particular activity or assignment or method of teaching improves students' learning, we need evidence to prove it, just as we do with our disciplinary research (Kreber, 2006).

The benefits and rewards for me to engage in SoTL are that it informs my teaching. It gives me the confidence to continue to develop and test new teaching strategies so I can reach the students and offer meaningful activities inside the classroom and on the clinical unit. My discipline is application-based; SoTL allows me to assess how that application is being seen and used by the students.
—DEBBIE, NURSING

Second, we have a responsibility as educators to contribute to the body of knowledge about effective teaching (Kreber, 2005). If we have tried a new teaching style and have evidence that it significantly improves student learning, then we ought to be sharing that with fellow educators. Of course, we probably do share this good news with local colleagues, but presenting at conferences and publishing in journals makes it more likely that your discovery will be used in classrooms other than your own. Contributing to scholarly knowledge about teaching and learning can inspire new ideas. How many times have you been to a conference or read a journal and came away with ideas for new projects, whether they be teaching or disciplinary? When we add to the scholarly body of knowledge about teaching and learning, we contribute to its growth and quality (Huber & Hutchings, 2005).

Third, it is likely no surprise that historically, research on teaching and learning has not been seen as especially credible (Weimer, 2006). Although we discuss this issue more in chapter 9, it is worthwhile to mention it here as well because it suggests a need to contribute to the scholarly literature on teaching and learning so that it becomes more credible. As Weimer (2006) states, "If practice is to improve and college teaching is to develop respect as a profession, there must be a viable literature associated with it" (p. 7). As dedicated teachers, it behooves us to accept this challenge and make efforts to contribute to this literature.

How to Use This Book

Following a discussion of the definitions and history of SoTL, the remaining chapters are set up so that you will work through each of the five steps of the SoTL process. These five steps are:

1. Generating a research question
2. Designing the study
3. Collecting the data
4. Analyzing the data
5. Presenting and publishing your SoTL project

Note that we are making a couple of assumptions. First, we assume that you know how to do research in your discipline, which may or may not be different from doing SoTL research (Bernstein, 2010). Second, we assume that you do not know very much about how to do a formal SoTL project. For some readers, one or both of these assumptions may be in error. Still, we hope you will gain some benefit in reading and thinking more deeply about SoTL and how our experiences and methods compare with your own.

Find a faculty learning community, find a mentor with some experience in SoTL, start a faculty/peer group so you can bounce ideas off one another to

look at SoTL. Attend a teaching/learning conference that is NOT discipline-specific. Some of my best ideas come from others who are using an activity in their disciplines but allow me to adapt it to my discipline and students. —DEBBIE, NURSING

Each chapter has two primary goals relating to the step in the SoTL process being covered. The first goal is to provide you with background information and resources for the research step. The background information includes a review of the literature and knowledge particular to each of the five steps. Also for each step, we include examples of SoTL studies to highlight particular aspects of the step. The second and primary goal of each chapter is to guide you through the research step for your own SoTL project. Toward that end, chapters 4 through 8 include a "workbook" that will guide you through a series of questions and smaller steps to help you think through and actually "do" each of the SoTL steps. We encourage you to respond to these workbook prompts in the workbook itself or to respond using the attached Word workbook pages. So that you are not completing these workbook pages without guidance, we have also completed a sample set of pages based on a study that Cathy Bishop-Clark and colleagues completed.

Role of Students

Obviously, students occupy a central role in SoTL. Most SoTL projects are designed with the goal of improving our teaching and enhancing student learning. In this sense, we engage in SoTL because of and for students. But there are ways to think about students' involvement in SoTL other than as "subjects" or "participants." Students can become collaborators or partners in all phases of a SoTL project, which is consistent with efforts to make teaching and learning more learner-centered. Trigwell and Shale (2004) argue that students have been largely absent in representations of SoTL. Yet we know that learner-centered instruction has been shown to enhance student learning (Tollefson & Osborn, 2008; Weimer, 2002), so there is good reason to think that including students as collaborators in SoTL not only will enhance learning for them, but also will likely improve SoTL work. For example, McKinney (2009) reports that students involved in SoTL on her campus describe being more connected to their courses, to their discipline, and to others. They also report being more engaged in their discipline and having more learner autonomy. Similarly, Werder and Otis (2010) report that many campuses are starting to involve their students in conversations about teaching and learning and also as collaborators in SoTL projects. Hutchings (2010) argues that efforts to include students in discussions about measuring learning serve to make them feel like "agents of their own learning."

In each chapter of this book, we discuss ideas about how to include students in the SoTL process, but we encourage you to start thinking now about involving students as collaborators in your SoTL projects. If you think about collaborations you've had with your colleagues on teaching or research projects, committees, and so on, how can some of those experiences translate to having students collaborate in your SoTL project? What similarities and differences will exist in the collaborative relationships? How might your SoTL project be enhanced by including students in the process?

2

Reflecting on Teaching and Learning

WHEN WE PUT OURSELVES in the position of trying to help students learn, we often think about why something worked or did not work; and then, in cases where something did not work, we try to think of ways to make it work (Witman & Richlin, 2007). We frequently question ourselves about what we do in the classroom and how it affects our students' learning, often trying to use the evidence we have available (e.g., performance on exams, student comments) to answer those questions (Savory, Burnett, & Goodburn, 2007). So we end up engaging in a thinking process that involves asking questions ("why didn't this work?"), forming hunches ("I think this did not work because the exercise was not scaffolded"), collecting information (students' performance on a revised activity), analyzing the information ("students' performance was much better than before"), and then possibly reporting that information (perhaps to students or colleagues). Although we may not have *explicitly* thought about all of these stages, we probably engage in some form of this process fairly often. If we didn't, then we likely would not grow as teachers. In fact, Chism (2008) suggests that there are several stages in a cycle of teacher growth. In the first stage, a teacher perceives an opportunity ("this activity worked really well so I think I will try using this format for additional activities") or a challenge ("this class discussion did not achieve the level of sophistication I wanted"). The second stage involves the teacher trying something new. In stage three, the teacher collects data, which he or she hopes will help to determine whether the change was effective. In stage four, the teacher reflects on the data to determine whether they had an impact on student learning. As we will see, these stages of teacher growth are similar to the steps in the SoTL process.

In this chapter, we briefly review the literature on reflecting on teaching and learning, including a discussion of the current "hot" topics in the learning literature. We also review the definitions and history of SoTL, including the standards of rigor of SoTL. Finally, we discuss how to do SoTL and introduce in some detail the five-step approach highlighted in this book.

To the extent that you spend time reflecting on your teaching and your students' learning, asking yourselves the previous questions, you are already engaged in the scholarship of teaching and learning (Robinson & Nelson, 2003; Saylor & Harper, 2003). The difference between what we do informally and what we do in SoTL rests on the formality of our reflections, observations, and sharing of our findings. Of course, our informal reflections and observations are valuable and likely go far toward making us good teachers (Brookfield, 2005; Kreber, 2006). But SoTL involves engaging in a more formal, albeit similar, process than reflecting on teaching. But before taking a closer look at the definitions, processes, and history of SoTL, let's look more carefully at the process of reflection, which is at the heart of SoTL (Gilpin & Liston, 2009; Hutchings, 2000; Kreber, 2006).

Scholars have been writing and thinking about reflection for a long time. Perhaps the most notable scholar to write about reflection was John Dewey. He identified several different types of thought, including belief, imagination, stream of consciousness, and reflection (1933), but the one that received the most attention was reflection. In an analysis of Dewey's writing, Rodgers (2002) describes the six phases of reflection. These include:

1. An experience
2. Spontaneous interpretation of the experience
3. Naming the problem(s) or the question(s) that arise out of the experience
4. Generating possible explanations for the problem(s) or question(s) posed
5. Using the explanations to devise full-blown hypotheses
6. Experimenting or testing the selected hypotheses

It is interesting to note that these phases closely mirror the questions posed in chapter 1 and, as we will shortly see, the steps of the SoTL research process. Schon (1983) presents another conceptualization of reflection, which characterizes reflection as a process in which a person tries to make sense of something while acting on it at the same time. The definition of *reflection* that we like is, "Reflection means thinking about what one is doing. It entails a process of contemplation with an openness to being changed, a willingness to learn, and a sense of responsibility for doing one's best" (Jay, 2003, p. 1). When we spend time reflecting on our teaching and students' learning, we try to do so with an open mind and with the expectation that such reflection will produce change.

If you doubt the importance of reflection in teaching and learning, consider the number of books written about reflecting on teaching and learning. Here is a small sampling: *Beyond the Books: Reflections on Learning and Teaching* (Hart, 1990), *Learning through Storytelling in Higher Education: Using Reflection & Experience to Improve Learning* (McDrury & Alterio, 2003), *Voices from the Classroom: Reflections on Teaching and Learning in Higher Education* (Newton, Ginsburg, Rehner, Rogers, Sbrizzi, & Spencer, 2001), *Developing Inquiry for Learning: Reflection, Collaboration and Assessment in Higher Education* (Ovens, Wells, Wallis, & Hawkins, 2011), *Educating the Reflective*

Practitioner: Toward a New Design for Teaching and Learning in the Professions (Schon, 1990).

As with reflection, much has been written about student learning. Here we highlight some of the current reflections and ideas about how students learn, which might serve as a source of ideas for your own SoTL project. Possibly starting with Bransford's (2000) book, *How People Learn*, there has been a shift to focus more on trying to understand *how* students learn and less on *what* they are learning. More recently, the physiological aspects of learning have taken center stage. Books such as *Brain Rules* (Medina, 2008), *Brain-Based Learning: The New Paradigm of Teaching* (Jensen & Jensen, 2008), and *Research-Based Strategies to Ignite Student Learning: Insights from a Neurologist and Classroom Teacher* (Willis, 2006) have highlighted physiological explanations for learning and provided tools that one can use to capitalize on this knowledge in the classroom. There are also new developments in the learner-centered paradigm. As we continue to move away from traditional and teacher-centered learning, there is much to discover and understand about our teaching and students' learning while we explore more learner-centered approaches (e.g., Doyle, 2008). Finally, interest continues in engaging students in multiple aspects of their learning (e.g., Black, 2010; Riggs, Gholar, & Gholar, 2009). For example, at our institution, we have redesigned our 25 most heavily enrolled courses to increase student engagement. Evaluations of the redesigned courses suggest that, as a result of introducing activities that engage students in their learning (e.g., working with other students on class projects or discussing ideas from readings outside of class with other students), students report that they learn more and are more satisfied with the course.

Before we begin to discuss in depth how our reflections on our teaching and students' learning can be transformed into SoTL, let's briefly review the history and definitions of SoTL as well some distinctions between SoTL and scholarly teaching.

I became interested in SoTL because I was looking for more objective ways to assess the effectiveness of my teaching, as well as to make my work more visible professionally. My students know how they have been impacted by my efforts, and find many ways of telling me so, but I hoped that SoTL would offer a way to bring my classroom work into an arena shared with colleagues. —MARY JANE, ENGLISH

Brief History and Definitions of SoTL

Much has been written about the history of SoTL (e.g., Bass, 1999; Healey, 2003; Huber & Hutchings, 2005; Kreber, 2005), so we offer only the highlights here. Although Ernest Boyer (1990) is rightly credited for laying the groundwork for SoTL, there were prior rumblings. For example, Cross (1986) argued that if teaching is going to be perceived as intellectually challenging, then it should include the same challenges as those in the research laboratory. Equating teaching and research gives credibility to our work in the classroom. Also in 1986, Chism and Sanders published an article on practice-centered inquiry, which essentially documented classroom research. This call encouraged teachers to start thinking about teaching and learning in a more scholarly manner.

In a well-known book, *Scholarship Reconsidered*, Boyer (1990) articulated four kinds of scholarship: the scholarship of integration, the scholarship of discovery, the scholarship of application, and the scholarship of teaching. Boyer's primary motivation for categorizing these four forms of scholarship was so they would achieve parity in their credibility and value, something he observed was missing in most institutions of higher learning. The last form of scholarship, of course, became known as SoTL. Glassick, Huber, and Maeroff (1997) followed Boyer's book with *Scholarship Assessed*, which essentially provided an update to *Scholarship Reconsidered* and was instrumental in articulating quality standards for SoTL (which we discuss later in this chapter). Eventually, organizations whose primary mission included SoTL, such as the Carnegie Academy for the Scholarship of Teaching and Learning (CASTL) and the International Society for the Scholarship of Teaching and Learning (ISSOTL), formed and continue to maintain a stronghold. In addition, several conferences focus on SoTL, including the Lilly Conferences, the International Conference on the Scholarship of Teaching and Learning, and SoTL Commons, and many disciplinary conferences have SoTL tracks. Numerous journals are now devoted to

SoTL, such as the *Journal of the Scholarship of Teaching and Learning, Mountain Rise, International Journal of the Scholarship of Teaching and Learning*, and the *Journal of Excellence in College Teaching*. In addition, many disciplines have their own journals devoted to SoTL, including *Chemical Educator, Teaching History*, and the *Journal of Nursing Education*. See appendices A and B for more detailed lists of SoTL conferences and journals.

As in any field, SoTL's 30-year history contains several shifts and changes, reflecting the growth of the field. In recent years, a push has been made toward being more theoretical so that we can explain students' learning rather than just describe it. Some argue that a theoretical approach will motivate us to understand the complexity of student learning (e.g., Hutchings & Huber, 2008; Kanuka, 2011). Examples of theories that have done justice to meeting this challenge include Perry's development scheme (Perry, 1970) and Baxter Magolda's Model of Epistemological Reflection (Baxter Magolda, 1999). Of course, adopting a more theoretical approach to SoTL allows us to build on knowledge to create a methodologically sound body of work. The push for more collaboration and integration (e.g., Stefani, 2011) is another current trend. As in many other disciplines, value is found in collaborating with other fields to provide an integrated perspective on teaching and learning. This idea is best articulated in Huber and Hutchings's (2005) teaching commons. Briefly, the teaching commons is a space in which educators collaborate and exchange ideas about teaching and learning with the goal of serving students' educational and personal needs. This idea is similar to Shulman's (2011) suggestion that SoTL is a hybrid, "sitting at the intersection of discipline and profession much like scholarship in medicine and nursing, law and environmental science" (p. 5).

On a similar note, Hutchings, Huber, and Ciccone (2011) advocate for an integrative vision for SoTL that focuses on the ways faculty embrace new teaching pedagogies, how professional development is articulated, the relationship between SoTL and assessment, and how institutions value and evaluate teaching. They argue that SoTL can have an impact on all of these areas, but it needs to focus on improving student learning. In fact, as we discuss later in this chapter, there is and has been more emphasis in SoTL on focusing on student learning. Similarly, Stefani (2011) suggests that SoTL should focus more on studying authentic learning and the skills and abilities that employers are seeking. Of course, there is greater emphasis on this kind of evaluation in assessment for accreditation as well.

Turning now to defining SoTL, in its 30-year history, numerous discussions and writings have taken place regarding the definition of SoTL. We will not try to present all of these here, but suffice it to say that it is clear that SoTL means different things to different people (e.g., Pan, 2009). To give you a few examples, Cross (1986) defined SoTL as "the study by classroom teachers of the impact of their teaching on the learning of the students in their classroom" (p. 3). Hutchings and Cambridge (1999) define SoTL as

> problem posing about an issue of teaching or learning, study of the problem through methods appropriate to the disciplinary epistemologies, application of results to practice, communication of results, self-reflection, and peer review. (p. 7)

In a study of those interested in SoTL, Healey (2003) found that 90% of respondents agree that SoTL "involves studying, reflecting on, and communicating about teaching and learning, especially within the context of one's discipline" (p. 14). Huber and Hutchings (2005) describe the four defining features of SoTL: questioning, gathering and exploring evidence, trying out and refining new thoughts, and going public. The definition or conceptualization of SoTL that we especially like is Shulman's (1999) attributes of SoTL. These are: "It becomes public; it becomes an object of critical review and evaluation by members of one's community; and members of one's community begin to use, build upon, and develop those acts of mind and creation" (p. 15).

It is important to make the distinction between the scholarship of teaching and learning and scholarly teaching. Witman and Richlin (2007) state that the purpose of scholarly teaching is to have an impact on teaching and learning, whereas SoTL results in a formal, peer-reviewed communication that becomes part of the larger knowledge base on teaching and learning. Hutchings and Shulman (1999) make a distinction among three different activities: excellent teaching, scholarly reflective teaching, and scholarship of teaching. They define *scholarly teaching* as

teaching that entails certain practices of classroom assessment and evidence gathering; teaching that is informed not only by the latest ideas in the field but by current ideas about teaching generally and specifically in the field; and teaching that invites peer collaboration or review. (p. 13)

There are also some distinctions in the literature among different types of SoTL. For example, Weimer (2006) classifies SoTL into two categories. The first, wisdom-of-practice scholarship, includes the experiences of teachers. Examples of wisdom-of-practice scholarship are personal accounts of change, recommended practices reports, recommended content reports, and personal narratives. The second, research scholarship, varies widely but can include quantitative investigations, qualitative studies, and descriptive research. Nelson (2003) describes five genres of SoTL, which are elaborated in chapter 3.

We mention these different definitions, conceptualizations, and types of SoTL, as well as related concepts such as "scholarly teaching," not to muddy the waters, but to suggest that such diversity can be productive and inclusive. We hope presenting this diversity assists you in identifying or creating a definition of SoTL that resonates with you and meets your needs.

I became interested in SoTL at an opening workshop on the regional campus as a new employee of Miami [University] and beginning in the tenure process. I knew I didn't want to do patient-based research, but my love is in teaching and my own lifelong learning so I knew SoTL could become my umbrella for scholarship. —DEBBIE, NURSING

Standards and Rigor of SoTL

As we already mentioned, research on teaching and learning has not always been seen as credible or rigorous (Weimer, 2006, 2008). This issue is worthy of discussion and is one that we take up in more detail in chapter 9 in our discussion of the reputation of SoTL and the challenges of doing SoTL. To summarize here, despite Boyer's (1990) call for equating the value of *all* forms of scholarship, the scholarship of teaching has not garnered the same respect as other forms of scholarship (Gurm, 2009). Even among those of us engaged in SoTL, some believe that the label "scholarship" should be restricted to those doing rigorous research of the sort found in conventional research journals (Bernstein, 2010). Of course, where one publishes SoTL and where one publishes "rigorous research" only deepens the chasm between SoTL and discipline-specific research (Gurung & Schwartz, 2010). Woodhouse (2010) describes the challenges of such a research-oriented model of SoTL by reminding us that classrooms are not research laboratories. Faculty cannot randomly assign students to conditions or control the conditions of their SoTL research in the same manner as they can in their disciplinary research. If teaching is to remain credible, then it ought to have a credible and respectable literature associated with it (Weimer, 2008).

We could spend a lot of time discussing and debating the various reasons for the reputation of research on teaching and learning, but for now, let's focus on the types of standards and rigor that are necessary to make quality contributions to the SoTL literature. There are two key issues. One is evaluating or judging whether a work is "scholarly." Diamond (1993) suggests that a work is scholarly if it possesses the following characteristics:

- Requires a high level of disciplinary expertise
- Charts new territory or is innovative
- Provides enough detail to be replicated
- Provides documentation of what was done and what was found
- Can be peer-reviewed
- Can be judged as being significant or impacting the discipline

Of course, meeting the criteria of a scholarly work is quite different from being good or rigorous work, which leads to the second key issue, which in turn most likely subsumes the first. This second issue is evaluating the quality and rigor of the work. We expect research in our disciplines to be rigorous and of high quality. We expect that any peer-reviewed journal we read or peer-reviewed conference presentation we attend is going to be of high quality. The same should be true about the scholarship on teaching and learning. But how do we ensure such high quality, particularly when SoTL cuts across all disciplines, which probably have their own idiosyncratic methods for judging quality and rigor? One of the earliest and perhaps most cited "standards of scholarly work" was articulated by Glassick et al. (1997). They propose the following six standards:

1. *Clear goals*: Are clear goals of the research articulated? Are these goals important?
2. *Adequate preparation*: Is there a demonstrable understanding of the literature? Does the scholar possess the skills necessary to conduct the research?
3. *Appropriate methods*: Does the scholar articulate methods appropriate to the stated goals?
4. *Significant results*: Were the goals of the research attained? Do the results make a significant contribution to the literature?
5. *Effective presentation*: Does the scholar effectively and appropriately communicate the results to the intended audience?
6. *Reflective critique*: Does the scholar critically evaluate the work in a manner that will improve the quality of the work?

If you compare these standards to those used in most disciplinary research, you will likely find many similarities. So making the transition from disciplinary research to SoTL is not necessarily a giant leap.

Savory et al. (2007) propose another method that can be used to evaluate the rigor of SoTL. Based on the six standards proposed by Glassick et al. (1997), Savory and colleagues include an assessment checklist in which a scholar indicates the extent of his or her agreement with such items as, "The hypothesis is an important question in need of an answer"; "Data-gathering methods are appropriate for testing the hypothesis"; and "The teacher brings an appropriate breadth of evidence to his or her critique."

Finally, in this era of new accreditation standards, we all probably have seen the push for accountability. At most institutions of higher education in the United States and abroad, departments and programs are being asked to articulate student learning outcomes and then to provide evidence that these learning outcomes are being achieved (e.g., Gordon, 2010; Marsh, 2007). Hutchings et al. (2011) argue that differences exist between assessment and SoTL. For example, assessment efforts are typically driven by external forces, while SoTL is usually motivated by curiosities about teaching and learning. The results of assessment are not peer-reviewed, nor are they made public in the same way as with SoTL. As such, you might find assessment efforts at odds with SoTL projects. Nonetheless, there is and can be an alignment between the two (Hutchings, 2010; Marsh, 2007). Assessment and SoTL are similar in that the purpose of each is to improve student learning. Gordon (2010), for example, has observed that when there is an alignment between SoTL and accountability, quality teaching practices are enhanced. This observation aligns with our own, that many SoTL and disciplinary teaching journals are shifting the standards for publication to exclude SoTL research that does not include measures of student learning.

Of course, the call for SoTL to focus on student learning is not new, nor is it necessarily driven by accreditation, accountability, and assessment. As we discussed previously, Hutchings and Shulman (1999) propose that SoTL should focus on student learning, and Trigwell and Shale (2004) propose a model of SoTL that is learner-centered and specifically includes students. More recently, Woodhouse (2010) argues for a model of SoTL that focuses explicitly on student learning. In a similar vein, in their analysis of the various "waves" of SoTL, Gurung and Schwartz (2010) call for the "third wave" to include a broader perspective of SoTL that involves investigations of factors that influence student learning. Our sense of this third wave is that SoTL that is publishable and considered rigorous will need to include actual evidence of student learning rather than, or in addition to, students' perceptions of learning, their attitudes, or their level of satisfaction, for example.

So is SoTL considered rigorous, scholarly work? Weimer's (2006) thoughtful analysis suggests that it is. First, she suggests that the mere number of new disciplinary journals devoted to research on teaching and learning (e.g., *Academy of Management Learning and Education*), as well as the increase in page numbers of already established journals (e.g., *Journal of Engineering Education*), attest to its growth. Second, the rejection rate of SoTL-type journals has increased. Third, journal editors are reporting that the standards for disciplinary journals devoted to research on teaching and learning are increasingly higher, as evidenced by their increased impact. Finally, several disciplinary journals devoted to teaching and learning are offering

recognition and rewards for best papers, again attesting to the drive to improve the quality of SoTL.

How to Do SoTL

Now that we have reviewed the history and definitions of SoTL, as well as the criteria for quality SoTL work, it is time to start thinking about your own SoTL project. The approach we take to doing SoTL is social science–based in nature, although we recommend and have adopted non–social science methodologies and approaches. As such, we recommend thinking of and engaging in SoTL using five steps. Chapters 4 through 8 document these steps in detail; here we provide an overview of what those steps look like.

1. *Generating the research question*: The goal of this step is to transform the hunches and ideas you've had about your teaching and student learning into research questions and hypotheses that can be answered empirically. As indicated in the beginning of this chapter, you probably already have these questions or hunches or hypotheses. For example, you might have wondered why your students did not seem to engage as much as you wanted in a class discussion about an important topic. Or you believe that the use of clickers in the classroom has increased participation levels among your students. The point of this first step is to take those questions and hunches and create interesting, meaningful, and measurable research questions.
2. *Designing the study*: The goal of this second step is to consider which type of research design best matches your research question. Basically, your research design will provide you with the mechanism with which to answer your research question.
3. *Collecting the data*: The goal of step three is to collect data that ideally will provide you with an answer to your question. It is likely that you've already thought about and used this step. For example, how do you know what works and what doesn't work in your classes? We use "data" (e.g., comments from students, performance on group projects or exams) from our students all the time to inform what

we do in class. In this step, we will make the process of data collection a little more systematic.

4. *Analyzing the data*: The goal of this step is to look carefully at the data and determine the answer to your research question. Again, this is likely a step with which you are familiar. How do you know that students did not achieve the intended learning outcomes? Perhaps because you recognized the puzzled looks on their faces when completing an activity, or maybe the level of critical thinking you expected to see in their papers was not apparent.

5. *Presenting and publishing your SoTL project*: The goal of this step is to share your research with peers at conferences and/or in journals. We all probably spend a lot of time talking with colleagues and students about teaching and learning. These conversations likely include seeking ideas about new teaching methods, talking about a technology that can enhance learning, or discussing something that happened in class that leaves us puzzled, for example. In this step, the goal is to report on the answer to your SoTL question to a larger audience and, ideally, contribute to the body of SoTL knowledge.

Those who want to publish in the SoTL field should either have expertise in social sciences and doing simple statistical analyses, or work in partnership with someone who has that expertise. Most interdisciplinary outlets for SoTL work seem to be biased toward the social science models, which are unfamiliar to me as a humanities expert. That said, engaging in SoTL is still very much worthwhile for professors in all fields for the new perspectives we can gain on our own teaching practices.
—MARY JANE, ENGLISH

3

Introduction to the Steps in the SoTL Research Process

THIS CHAPTER BEGINS to provide the types of examples we hope will help you to visualize how you can apply SoTL research in your own classroom. We begin with a recent situation in which we felt that our students were not learning a particular concept well. The concept was a relatively introductory idea in computer science—repetition. We were teaching the structure of a "do while" loop. Used in computer programs, looping structures allow a section of code to be repeated many times. Students consistently scored poorly on the quiz following this one-week unit and each semester they seemed to miss the very same questions. Not only were quiz scores low, but we would observe students walk out of the classroom and tell their friends, "I'll be glad when this unit is over. I hardly understood any of it. I hope I never see this stuff again." Even though lectures were carefully planned and included examples of the mistakes students were likely to make, they still made the very same mistakes when working on problems independently. We were as frustrated with our experience as the students were with theirs and wanted to improve student understanding of the content as well as their attitudes about the topic.

We decided to incorporate a variation of the Think-Pair-Share (Lyman, 1981; Millis & Cottell, 1998) into the class sessions related to this particular looping structure. For each class session, we posed a brief question, and students were given about 5 minutes to solve the problem independently. Next, students were asked to talk about the problem with one other person in the class, comparing solutions and identifying any logic errors they may have made. Finally, the instructor reviewed the solution. Rather than lecture, class sessions consisted of the following steps:

- short explanation,
- independent work,
- shared work, and
- discussion of solutions.

Each problem took 10–15 minutes to cover in total. To determine whether the use of Think-Pair-Share led to increased learning, we gave students the same quiz that we had used in prior semesters. The quiz was a simple 10-point, multiple-choice instrument consistent in form and format with the other quizzes given throughout the term. After we gave the quiz, we determined the average quiz grade and compared that to the average of quizzes in prior classes where we did not use the Think-Pair-Share method. Our students did so much better on the quiz (compared to previous semesters) that we asked our department chair to put us on the agenda at the next department meeting to discuss using this particular technique in our classrooms.

This simple illustration is typical of virtually all good teachers' experiences. We either notice or feel that something is just not leading to the learning we would like. In this case there were obvious indicators: poor quiz scores and verbal comments as students walked out the door. We try a different technique

(Think-Pair-Share), evaluate it in some way (a quiz, a test, or an observation), and then discuss with a group of colleagues what we tried. We reflect on what worked, we modify what we did, or we abandon our approach entirely and try something else.

It is important to note that learning and teaching are incredibly complex and the methods to study teaching and learning are equally varied and complex. We identify a five-step process in our SoTL work to simplify what can initially seem to be an overwhelming and daunting task—studying the teaching and learning environment. And we use the example we describe previously to show the similarity in SoTL work to the work you may already do in the classes you teach.

We can look at the previous example in light of this five-step approach as follows:

Step 1: Identify the research question. In the previous illustration, the research question is, "Will use of the Think-Pair-Share technique improve understanding of the 'do while' loop?"

Step 2: Design the study. In this case, the design of the study was to try a new technique, give a quiz, and then compare that quiz to prior quizzes when the learning technique was not used.

Step 3: Collect the data. As is typical in most college classrooms, learning is measured by some kind of exam or quiz. In this case, a quiz that was used in previous terms was our measure of learning, and data collection occurred when we gave the quiz and then graded responses.

Step 4: Analyze the data. Our fourth step in this example was simply to determine the mean quiz grade and compare this mean with previous results.

Step 5: Present and publish your SoTL project. In our illustration, we talked about the project at a scheduled department meeting.

Having this guided five-step process promoted confidence in each step. I was able to communicate my concerns and validate expected outcomes to my mentors and peers. If I didn't have this five-step process, my project would have mushroomed into something that probably would not have offered meaningful results in the end. —DEBBIE, NURSING

Most of us interested in student learning have experienced some variation of the steps previously outlined in the courses we teach. The difference between what good teachers already do and a SoTL project is that SoTL projects are well defined, carefully and systematically studied, and put in the context of others' research, and the results are shared with a broader community. Unlike the example we illustrate, SoTL work must be grounded in existing literature. Rather than start from scratch, we learn what others have published in both Think-Pair-Share and the teaching of the "do while" loop statement. Like we do in our disciplinary research, in SoTL we build on the work others have published and subject our work to rigorous peer review. Table 3.1 provides an overview of each step and gives a very high level comparison of the differences between evaluating your everyday classroom in informal ways and conducting a SoTL study. The five steps of this process provide the framework for the next five chapters.

This five-step process is very similar to the steps of inquiry of the scientific method: construct a hypothesis, test the hypothesis, analyze results, and report results. For simplicity we describe the SoTL process in five discrete steps. In reality, we may move from one step to the next and then back to the first step. For instance, we may identify the research question and then revise that question as we design the study. Similarly, it may be that we designed the SoTL project to be entirely quantitative with numerical data only, but as we collect that data we realize that additional interviews with students might add much to our understanding of how students learn.

Even though the idea of SoTL was new to me, the five steps made the process doable and less intimidating to me. —MICHELLE, PSYCHOLOGY

Identify the Research Question

We have hundreds, if not thousands, of questions about our students' learning and about our teaching. We question whether the exam we created was a good measure of the learning we wanted to evaluate. We ask why our evening section was so much more engaged than our morning section when the content was virtually the same. We observe that students appear to be graduating from our department as very nonreflective

TABLE 3.1 Illustration of Steps in a SoTL Study		
	SoTL Pilot Study	*SoTL Project*
Identify the Research Question	Will this new teaching technique (the Think-Pair-Share method) help students understand the "do while" loop?	Review prior research and put this question in the context of other work in this area. Clearly identify how this question builds on the work of others in either the Think-Pair-Share method or what is known about teaching the "do while" loop. Research how learning will be measured and state the research question in clear and measurable terms.
Design the Study	Use the Think-Pair-Share technique, observe how it goes, see how students do on a subsequent quiz, and compare those quiz scores to scores in previous years when the Think-Pair-Share was not used.	Identify the best research approach to answer the question at hand. Observe and record learning using the Think-Pair-Share technique in a careful and systematic way. Identify how to measure student learning and what aspects of learning will be measured. Consider using a pre-test to document a baseline of knowledge. If possible, consider teaching two sections of the same course. In one section use the Think-Pair-Share technique; in the other do not. Measure knowledge before and after the unit of study.
Collect the Data	Use the same quiz as last term.	Research whether standardized and validated instruments exist in the field to measure learning in the particular area. If not, design an instrument. Before using the instrument in the course, pilot it. Use existing literature, colleagues, and students to help create or identify an instrument that is both reliable and valid.
Analyze the Data and Draw Conclusions	Compare the mean score of the quiz using the Think-Pair-Share with the mean score in previous terms when the Think-Pair-Share technique was not used.	If the data are quantitative and a pre- and post-test design was used, use an appropriate statistical test to compare whether the measure of content knowledge is significantly different from the pre-test to the post-test.
Present and Publish Your SoTL Project	Discuss the experience in the faculty lounge or in a department meeting.	Present the results of the SoTL study in a peer-reviewed journal or at a conference, relating the work to the existing work on the effectiveness of Think-Pair-Share.

learners and we question whether there is something systematic that we could implement as a department to improve such reflection.

SoTL questions are not always about our own classrooms. Some of the more influential SoTL studies involve multiple sections, courses, departments, or institutions (e.g., Treisman, 1992). For instance, you may be interested in whether a series of courses influences outcomes at the end of a college career. Colleagues can work together to study questions in multidisciplinary or multi-institutional ways. Whether your question is about a technique you used in your own classroom or whether it is multi-institutional, the question you identify will define and guide the other aspects of your project.

An essential part of all scholarly inquiry is to put the research question in the context of what has been previously done. Scholars in all disciplines begin by understanding what has been done in the field. Unlike much of the literature in your disciplinary work, the literature relevant to your SoTL research question can span multiple disciplines.

Identifying a research question can be daunting and overwhelming simply because of the vast number of possibilities. But such possibilities can be considered an advantage. Teaching and learning is interesting—incredibly interesting. And the first step of the SoTL process is to identify which of the many interesting questions we are committed to and interested in studying and also needs studying so the entire field can progress. Like the previous illustrations, the questions often stem from experiences in our own classroom. Often, SoTL research questions are inspired by those experiences and observations. One of the exciting aspects of SoTL questions is that they tend to be practical and applied, and have direct implications for the classes we teach.

Design the Study

The research question will influence all of the other steps in your process, including the specific strategies you will use to answer your question. The strategies for answering your question generally fall into two categories: quantitative and qualitative. In very general terms, quantitative designs tend to incorporate questionnaires, tests, or existing databases, whereas qualitative designs tend to incorporate observations, interviews, or focus groups (Frechtling & Westat, 1997).

Consider the groups you want to study, how many students you will study, and whether you will use comparison groups. Often the answers to these questions will be determined by practical constraints. For instance, you may have a class size of 25 and your project must be within your class. But consider whether your colleagues teaching the same class would be willing to participate and whether your questions demand the use of a comparison group. In our Think-Pair-Share example, our study became much more powerful when we compared the outcomes of the same learning unit to results when the Think-Pair-Share method was not used.

As you design your individual SoTL study, see if it makes sense to put it in the context of a larger personal research agenda. In our example we may want to know if Think-Pair-Share leads to better understanding of a concept over the course of a semester. However, we could create a first study that is smaller in scale. For instance, the first study could investigate whether the Think-Pair-Share technique led to improved learning in one class session. Subsequent studies could then look at whether the Think-Pair-Share

technique (when used consistently) leads to improved learning over the course of a semester. As a general guideline, design a pilot study that is simple, and then build on that study.

Learning about study design was most helpful to me; my first ideas were all rather complicated and hard to execute, but going through the steps, along with the examples provided for each one, helped me understand how to design a simple study that would be informative but easier to execute than the study I originally designed. I really needed to see concrete examples to have a clear idea of my options for SoTL studies. —MARY JANE, ENGLISH

Collect the Data

As educators, we collect data when we grade homework assignments, give quizzes, grade examinations, evaluate classroom presentations, survey students, and administer final course evaluations. We evaluate the engagement of our students by observing their class participation, noticing their body language, and watching their eyes as we explain a complicated topic. Not only do we collect data at a classroom level, but at the department level we collect data about the number of graduates, the time to graduation, the courses that are most often dropped, the mean evaluations of all teachers in the department, and job placement rates for graduates. Data are also collected at an institution level: the percentage of minority students and the retention, average age, and average GPA of our students are reported for state and national assessment. Data drive many decisions in our classroom, our department, and our institution.

With SoTL projects, there are many different ways to collect data, and the research question and design drive the kind of data we collect and the manner in which we collect it. In our Think-Pair-Share example, the data we collected were from a quiz.

Analyze the Data

The kind of analysis you will do depends on the question you asked and the design you created. If you asked a question that was quantitative in nature, you are likely to answer the question using statistics, which may be as simple as the average quiz grade and the distribution of the grades, or it may be a more formal statistical test, such as a *t*-test to determine the significance of the results. Alternatively, your data analysis may involve qualitative data, which requires sifting through data looking for patterns or themes.

The most fun was finally seeing the results and having my hypothesis supported. I also hand-calculated my chi-square, which was fun for me as a long-standing qualitative researcher. —GINA, SOCIOLOGY

Present and Publish Your SoTL Work

The final step in our five-step process is making your study available to a larger audience. In fact, it is not only the final step, but going public is also one of the necessary conditions for your SoTL project to be considered scholarship. In the previous illustration, the work was made public on a very small scale—that is, it was introduced to the department. In most academic institutions, the work will not yet be considered scholarship. In general, SoTL needs to be reported beyond our own department or institution. Publications and presentations are the traditional outlets for such work. SoTL work can be published in journals within the field such as *Computer Science Education* or *Teaching of Psychology*. Most likely there is at least one, if not several, discipline-specific journal appropriate for your study. Similarly, many are more general in nature such as the *Journal of Excellence in College Teaching* and *College Teaching*. Presentations can be made to local, regional, national, or international audiences. Venues are typically available within your discipline, and more general teaching and learning conferences are available to a variety of disciplines. Where you target your work depends on the nature of your SoTL study.

SoTL presentations usually have an audience from diverse backgrounds and so encourage interdisciplinary and integrative thinking and discussions. Scientific conference audiences generally are more discipline-centered. I find [that] SoTL conferences engender participants to engage in a more transformational way of thinking and discussing. —ALAN, ZOOLOGY

Illustrations

To further illuminate this five-step process, we outline several examples of SoTL projects to illustrate a range of SoTL investigations. In the examples we choose, the results are very practical and applied and are often immediately useful. The results help us understand whether our everyday teaching activities lead to increased learning. For each illustration, we begin by describing a SoTL project. Following the description, we provide a brief illustration of what was done at each step. Keep in mind that, at this point, the idea is to move you in the direction of creating your own SoTL project. We explore the details of each step in more detail in subsequent chapters.

Illustration 1: How Novice Programmers Program

Early in Cathy Bishop-Clark's career, she was teaching a course in introductory programming. She was having a difficult time understanding why so many students could not grasp the very fundamental constructs of program design. She learned from quizzes and tests that students would frequently come up with programming solutions that were not even close to a correct answer. In many cases, she could not begin to guess what they were thinking as they attempted to solve the problem.

To help her understand what students were thinking, she used a protocol analysis, a method in which students are asked to think aloud as they process information or solve problems (Crutcher, 1994; Simon & Caplan, 1989). The students are not explaining or analyzing the process of their thinking; rather, they are simply verbalizing every thought that occurs. In this case the student verbalized as she went about solving a computer programming problem. Cathy's only role was to prompt the student to continue talking aloud as she solved the problem.

To gain insight into the challenges her students were experiencing, Cathy studied the literature on novice and expert problem solving. Differences between novice and expert problem solving have been studied in many areas, including chess, physics, electronics, and programming. Cathy was interested in better understanding the thought process of her students as they solved what most in the field would consider very simple problems. She was only mildly interested in whether a solution was correct; rather she wanted to describe and identify some of the problem-solving behaviors of novices. She was interested in what students thought about when they created such a solution. In essence, she wanted a window to the student's cognitive processing. Using the technique of protocol analysis, she audiotaped a 30-minute session, transcribed the session, and analyzed it. She analyzed the protocol with a particular focus on characteristics identified in the literature as being "novice traits" (Bishop-Clark, 1992).

This study can be considered exploratory and descriptive. The study described "what is"—that is, it helped Cathy understand an individual student's current processing. The analysis consisted of identifying what themes emerged as she transcribed the tapes and used literature to explain those themes. This particular

study led to a tremendous amount of insight, which continues to serve her well 20 years after the study. She learned about how students represented the problem, planned a solution, and carried out the plan, and how their knowledge was organized (Bishop-Clark, 1992). Table 3.2 maps this SoTL project to the five-step process.

Illustration 2: Comparing Understanding of Concepts Using Two Different Techniques

Our first illustration involved studying a single student as she talked aloud while she wrote a computer program. The emphasis was on gaining an in-depth understanding of a single student, and the SoTL study was largely descriptive and qualitative. Our second illustration involves comparing learning at the end of

TABLE 3.2 How Novice Programmers Write Programs	
Identify the Research Question	What does a novice programmer think as she solves simple computer programs?
Design the Study	**What groups do you want to study?** Cathy did not study a group; instead she studied a single person. **How many people will you study?** One. **Will you do a pilot?** No. **Where will you conduct the study?** The study was conducted at the campus library. **Will you use comparison groups?** No; because of practical constraints, Cathy studied a single program and a single student. **What kinds of outcomes do you expect?** Cathy expected to have additional insight into the process a student follows when solving a simple computer programming problem.
Collect the Data	**What data will you collect?** Audio recording of a student as she talked aloud while solving a simple computer programming problem. **When will you collect them?** Immediately after a concept was introduced but before the student had practiced it. **Who will collect the data?** The teacher of the course. **Why are you collecting these data?** To better understand how a novice programmer thinks as she solves a computer programming problem.
Analyze the Data and Draw Conclusions	**How will you analyze the data?** Data will be transcribed and studied to identify whether certain themes emerge. **If your data set needs to be coded, who will code it?** The data need to be transcribed, and the researcher will do it.
Report the Findings	**Where do you plan to present your findings?** Local/regional conference focused on computer science education. **Where do you plan to publish your findings?** *Computer Science Education.*

a semester in which two different approaches were used. The goal of the second illustration is to identify whether a new approach to teaching works better than a traditional approach. This particular study was larger in scope, involved more time, and included a pilot study.

At the time of the study, Cathy Bishop-Clark's department was considering moving to a new computer programming language. The new language was very visual and used symbols (visual BASIC); the old was text-based (quick BASIC). Rather than adopt the change without data, the department tested students' understanding of concepts at the end of the term. Some faculty in the department taught using the traditional technique (text), others used the new technique (visual), and those data were compared.

Two key elements were involved in this study: identification of the fundamental concepts and development of an instrument to measure understanding of those concepts. Fortunately, the key concepts of the course were clearly articulated in the course syllabus. Unfortunately, no standardized instrument existed with which to measure those concepts.

Prior to this study, a pilot study was used to develop the instrument that measured students' understanding of the course's fundamental concepts. In the pilot study, faculty and students gave detailed feedback on the instrument in the form of interviews. Additionally, 73 students completed the instrument. Two students were hired to rate correctness of responses for every item on the pilot quiz. As a result of pre-testing our instrument, we eliminated two questions and ended up with a nine-item quiz (all open-ended questions). The goal of the pilot study was simply to create an instrument (a quiz) that accurately measured students' understanding of the fundamental concepts of the course.

After the quiz was developed and tested, the results from two groups of students were compared after taking a semester course in computer programming. Both groups took the same course; however, the first group took the course using the traditional teaching technique (text-based) and the second took the course using the new technique (visual). Several different classes and instructors participated in the study. The course was standard enough that the same quiz could be given in each section.

The study indicated that for certain questions, students using the visual language performed better on the quiz than students who used the text-based language. For other questions, students in both groups had similar scores. But in no case did the students using the text-based language perform better than those using the visual language. The data gleaned from this SoTL study led to the department's adoption of the visual language. In this example, SoTL work had implications beyond a particular classroom; it led to a change in the department. The department was ahead of its time. Within a few years, most of the field had made this switch (Bishop-Clark, 1998).

Undergraduate students were involved in this SoTL project at various phases. Students were hired to grade the quizzes in both the pilot study and the study that compared the two different learning techniques. Students were involved in creating and grading the quiz and helped with the statistical analysis. Table 3.3 summarizes this SoTL project.

Illustration 3: Reporting on 10 Years of Experiences and Results of Using Peer Instruction in Physics Courses

Our first example involved studying a single student as she talked aloud while she solved a simple problem. The emphasis was on gaining an in-depth understanding of the cognitive processing of a single student. This SoTL project can be considered a "what is" project. In other words, we described in detail what the processing of a single student looks like. It is qualitative and descriptive. The time frame for the first example was a single two-hour session. The second example involved comparing learning at the end of a semester in a course in which two programming languages (one visual and one text) were used. The length of time for this example was two semesters: one to create the learning instrument and one to run the study. The objective was to identify whether using a new visual programming language would lead to different levels of mastery than using a traditional text-based language. The final illustration (see Table 3.4) is similar to the second in that new techniques are introduced. In this case, however, the course of interest was an introductory physics course. Like the second example, an innovative teaching technique—Peer Instruction—was used. But unlike the second example, the authors modified the specifics of Peer Instruction each year over a period of 10 years and monitored how those changes influenced student learning. This final example illustrates how some SoTL projects turn

TABLE 3.3 Comparing Understanding of Concepts Taught Using Two Different Techniques	
Identify the Research Question	Will students using a visual language better understand the fundamental concepts of the course than those using a text-based language?
Design the Study	**What groups do you want to study?** Two groups: the first group took a class using a visual language; the second group took the class using a text-based language. **How many people will you study?** About 30–40 in each group. **Will you do a pilot?** We used a pilot study to develop the instrument we used to measure understanding of fundamental concepts. **Where will you conduct the study?** The study was conducted in the classroom. **Will you use comparison groups?** There were two groups in this study: one group used a graphic language and the other used a text-based language. **What kinds of outcomes do you expect?** We expected the students using the visual language to have a better understanding of fundamental concepts than those using the text language.
Collect the Data	**What data will you collect?** Responses to a nine-question, open-ended quiz that was developed through the pilot study to evaluate understanding of key programming concepts. **When will you collect them?** At the end of the semester. **Who will collect the data?** The researchers. **Why are you collecting these data?** To help understand whether the choice of programming language affects learning.
Analyze the Data and Draw Conclusions	**How will you analyze the data?** Two different coders will code accurate responses on a 1–4 point scale for the nine questions. **If your data set needs to be coded, who will code it?** Two students were hired to code the correctness of the nine questions.
Report the Findings	**Where do you plan to present your findings?** We planned to present at a local/regional conference focused on computer science education. **Where do you plan to publish your findings?** We planned to present in a discipline-related journal focused on educational issues.

into a program of study that can span a decade or longer.

Catherine Crouch and Eric Mazur (2001) studied Harvard students taking a calculus-based introductory physics course and an algebra-based introductory physics course for nonmajors. They and several of their colleagues used a technique called Peer Instruction (PI), which is different from traditional lecture. The basic framework for a class taught with PI is as follows:

1. Students are given a short presentation by the instructor.

2. Students then take a ConcepTest, a short, multiple-choice instrument that probes understanding of the idea presented.
3. Students form individual answers and submit their answers to the instructor.
4. Students then discuss their answers and convince one another that their answer is correct.
5. Students have a chance to change their responses, and the instructor again polls the students for their responses.

The authors found that, once they moved to a PI format, students' understanding of the course mate-

TABLE 3.4 Reporting on 10 Years of Experience	
Identify the Research Question	Do students using Peer Instruction (PI) in algebra- and calculus-based introductory physics courses increase mastery of conceptual reasoning and quantitative problem solving?
Design the Study	**What groups do you want to study?** Students at Harvard University taking calculus- and algebra-based introductory physics courses. **How many people will you study?** Over a period of seven years, approximately 1,500 students. **Will you do a pilot study?** In the traditional sense of the word, no "pilot" study was performed; however, each year, the study built on the findings from the previous year. **Where will you conduct the study?** The authors conducted the study in a classroom setting. **Will you use comparison groups?** Students using PI from 1991 to 2000 were studied. Data were collected from students using traditional instruction in 1990 and were used for comparison. **What kinds of outcomes do you expect?** The authors expected to see increased mastery of conceptual reasoning and quantitative problem solving as they refined their implementation of the PI strategy.
Collect the Data	**What data will you collect?** Data to evaluate student learning, including scores on two standard tests (Force Concept Inventory and Mechanics Baseline Test), traditional examination questions, and ConceptTests. **When will you collect them?** The beginning of the term, throughout the class, and at the end of the term. **Who will collect the data?** The instructors of the course. **Why are you collecting these data?** To identify whether PI and subsequent improvement leads to improved understanding.
Analyze the Data and Draw Conclusions	**How will you analyze the data?** A variety of statistical tests. **If your data set needs to be coded, who will code it?** The data do not need to be coded.
Report the Findings	**Where do you plan to present your findings?** It is not clear whether the authors intended to present their findings. **Where do you plan to publish your findings?** *American Journal of Physics.*

rial improved. They measured both conceptual reasoning and quantitative problem solving using a variety of measures. They were able to use two standard tests: the Force Concept Inventory (FCI) test (Hestenes, Wells, & Swackhammer, 1992) and the Mechanics Baseline Test (MBT) (Hestenes & Wells, 1992). The FCI test was given as a pre- and post-test; the MBT was given only as a post-test. Additionally, the authors included traditional examination questions on common exams. Finally, a conceptual question, called a ConcepTest, was used both in the classroom during the PI and on examinations. In short, the authors used four different measures to evaluate understanding.

One of the reasons this particular study was chosen as an illustration is because of the long-term nature of the study. The results of 10 years of studying classes are presented, and over the years the authors improved implementation of the PI. Over the decade substantial changes were incorporated and the impact of each change was documented. In other words, the authors found that the first change improved scores.

Therefore, two years later they added a second feature, which improved scores even more.

To summarize, several strengths of this particular SoTL study should be noted. First, a total of five instructors used PI beginning in 1991, so the results are not dependent on a single instructor's style. Second, the authors measured understanding based on four different measures, all of which pointed to the same outcome—increased learning. Third, this particular example is an excellent illustration of a long-term study in which the PI was modified in ways that improved students' understanding. That improvement and those changes were systematically studied over a decade. Table 3.4 summarizes this SoTL project.

Practical Constraints

In a perfect world, we would have unlimited time and resources to investigate our SoTL project, but in practice we are pulled in many different directions. Therefore, practical constraints must be considered when identifying your SoTL project.

How much time do you have to devote to this investigation? If you are an academic, you have teaching, research, and service obligations. Consider whether you will have the time to investigate the question you pose. If you do not, consider making the question smaller and the design simpler. For instance, rather than investigating whether your students improved their critical thinking over the course of a semester, consider investigating whether they improved their critical thinking for a single assignment.

Is your investigation publishable? To determine whether the investigation is publishable, see whether other similar investigations have been published. If they have, and there are still questions in your area, then the answer is probably yes. Additionally, consider the "norms" in your field. If you work in a highly quantitative field, it is likely that SoTL work with a quantitative aspect will be more publishable than one that is entirely qualitative. Nontenured faculty should consider whether this project will help them achieve tenure and, if not, they must weigh the consequences of putting time and energy into something that may not contribute to the tenure process.

Is the scope of your project reasonable? As a first step, make your research question smaller rather than larger, focused rather than general, narrow rather than broad. Consider whether you have the time, resources, and energy to answer the question you would like to investigate. If you do not, before you abandon the idea entirely, see if you can make the question smaller, more focused, and narrower.

Is there funding to support your project? In addition to external funding agencies, many colleges and universities have internal support for SoTL projects. While this funding is not typically on the scale of externally funded grants, it also does not require the same amount of accountability, which can be very time-consuming in externally funded projects.

Does this SoTL project tie into your teaching and service interests? Some of the best SoTL projects are ones that tie together research, teaching, and service. In a recent learning community we led, one of our participants designed a SoTL project that investigated the impact service learning had on her nursing students. She began a research line related to service learning in nursing. Additionally, she became the nursing department's expert in service learning and used that expertise to assist other faculty in her department. She effectively combined her SoTL project with her teaching, research, and service interests.

Involving Students

Students can play an active role in virtually all aspects of SoTL work. Recall that SoTL is the acronym for the Scholarship of Teaching *and* Learning. Who better to inform us about the learning process than students? Students can become part of every aspect of the investigation of teaching and learning. They can be hired to help survey the literature, enter data, code transcripts, identify the research question, help design the study, and analyze results.

Not only can students be hired to assist in various phases of your SoTL project, they also can become partners and coresearchers in your project. By inviting students to become partners in the research process and by giving them more responsibility at every phase, we are developing them as independent learners and are engaging them in an important educational process—the work of discovery.

In their edited collection, *Engaging Student Voices in the Study of Teaching and Learning*, Werder and Otis (2009) present a collection of essays that outline the many different ways students can become active participants in SoTL work. This volume of work includes chapters that explore the theoretical dimensions of including students in the work of teaching and learning and others that focus on the practical dimensions. Students can be part of one aspect of the SoTL process (such as trained observers) or they can become partners in the entire SoTL process. By including students as partners in the process, your SoTL project can be richer, more rewarding, and stronger. Consider early and often whether and how students can participate in your SoTL work.

Creating Your SoTL Plan Worksheet

The following is the worksheet we've designed to take you a step further as you design your SoTL project. Briefly respond to the questions in each category. Do not be concerned if you do not have a clear vision of each answer. Instead, use the worksheet to help you begin to understand the aspects of the project you should begin to think about.

Identify the Research Question	Clearly and succinctly identify the research question.
Design the Study	What groups do you want to study? How many people will you study? Will you do a pilot? Where will you conduct the study? Will you use comparison groups? What kinds of outcomes do you expect?
Collect the Data	What data will you collect? When will you collect them? Who will collect the data? Why are you collecting these data?
Analyze the Data and Draw Conclusions	How will you analyze the data? If your data set needs to be coded, who will code it?
Report the Findings	Where do you plan to present your findings? Where do you plan to publish your findings?

Creating Your SoTL Plan: Completed Worksheet

Chapters 3 through 7 illustrate an example regarding one of our SoTL projects (Bishop-Clark, Courte, Evans, & Howard, 2007). In this study, the use of an innovative programming language in an introductory computing class was studied from both a quantitative and qualitative perspective. More than 150 students in an introductory computing class participated in a 2.5-week unit to learn programming through the graphical programming environment of Alice. Students were surveyed before and after their experience. They completed a questionnaire about their enjoyment and confidence, along with a content test of their understanding of fundamental computer programming concepts. Additionally, students participated in one of three focus groups and were asked to write an essay requiring them to reflect on their experience. We chose this particular example as a continuing illustration in the next four chapters because of the variety of measures used and the relative simplicity of the concept. In essence, an innovative teaching approach is studied among multiple dimensions: confidence, enjoyment, and achievement. Additionally, this example illustrates a SoTL project that uses both quantitative and qualitative measures. We've completed the SoTL worksheet for this project as an additional example of how you might conceptualize your project.

Identify the Research Question	**Clearly and succinctly identify the research question.**
	 There were three research questions:
	     Will students increase their confidence in programming after a 2.5-week session using Alice?
	     Will students increase their enjoyment of programming after a 2.5-week session using Alice?
	     Will students improve their knowledge of programming after a 2.5-week session using Alice?

Design the Study	**What groups do you want to study?** We studied students taking an introductory liberal education computer science course. **How many people will you study?** Approximately 150 students in multiple sections of the same course. **Will you do a pilot?** We did do a pilot to develop the questions we used to measure confidence, enjoyment, and knowledge and to identify any unexpected issues. **Where will you conduct the study?** In the classroom during a 2.5-week session. **Will you use comparison groups?** No. **What kinds of outcomes do you expect?** We expected students to increase confidence, enjoyment, and knowledge of programming after the Alice experience.
Collect the Data	**What data will you collect?** Three instruments were developed: one to measure confidence, one to measure enjoyment, and one to measure knowledge. **When will you collect them?** We administered the instruments before the 2.5-week unit and again after the 2.5-week unit. **Who will collect the data?** The instructors teaching the course.
Analyze the Data	**How will you analyze the data?** We primarily used t-tests. **If your data set needs to be coded, who will code it?** We hired students to code the essays.
Report the Findings	**Where do you plan to present your findings?** A national conference in computing education. **Where do you plan to publish your findings?** We targeted the *Journal of Educational Computing Research.*

4

Generating the Research Idea

THE FIRST STEP in the process of SoTL research is to identify the research question. A carefully crafted research question takes time, a thoughtful analysis of your own interests and practical constraints, a thorough review of the literature, and feedback from trusted colleagues. Such a process is iterative and moves from broad to specific. In fact, clearly articulating the research question is one of the most important steps you will take in your investigation. The research question you identify will influence the kinds of methods you will use, the numbers of students you will need to involve in your study, and the data collection techniques you will use. Light, Singer, and Willett (1990) explain that well-crafted questions guide the systematic planning of research. Formulating your questions precisely allows you to design a study with a good chance of answering them.

Your research questions come first from the experiences in your classroom that you find intriguing. Hundreds if not thousands of interesting and sometimes unexplainable phenomena occur in our classrooms. Why did my students fail to learn even the basic principles in a 16-week course? Does engaging in reflective writing lead to deep and sustained learning? Why did I have a lively and engaging dialogue in my 10:00 a.m. class but a completely dull and uninteresting conversation on the very same topic with my 11:30 a.m. class? Are there systematic differences among those who perform well in my classes compared to those who do not succeed? Chances are you

will not have a problem identifying interesting aspects of your classroom. The bigger challenge will be reducing those interesting observations to a clear and articulate question or set of questions.

The general area that you wish to investigate can be labeled the "research theme." Once you have identified the research theme, you need to begin to narrow the theme to a specific set of questions. Some questions will remain somewhat vague and in fact will look very similar to the general theme. For instance, if your question involves understanding *how* a student learns, it may be difficult to narrow your question. This is especially true if you do not want to test a specific theory but prefer to remain open to all of the possibilities. However, with many questions you will be able to move from a general theme to a very specific and testable question. Moving to as specific a question as possible is the goal.

The most difficult part of identifying the research question was narrowing it down to a workable project. There was so much to explore, so much that was interesting. The challenge was to bring it all down to a single, workable question. The idea for my question came out of a particular frustration of mine. My students complained more about writing in classes than anything else, even exams, so I wanted to explore what was really at the heart of their complaints. I wanted to

make the experience more enjoyable for them.
—MICHELLE, PSYCHOLOGY

Categorizing Research Questions

In her introduction to *Opening Lines: Approaches to the Scholarship of Teaching and Learning* (2000), Pat Hutchings details a taxonomy of four types of questions that help define and clarify SoTL research. It is important to understand that these categories are in no way mutually exclusive but instead may provide a structure to begin thinking about your own SoTL questions. The first kind of question is "what works." Many of the questions we have investigated over the years fall into this category and this is often the starting point for SoTL work. We often want to find evidence for the effectiveness of some new approach that we are trying in the classroom. The second kind of question is "what is," and in this category the focus is on describing "what it looks like." The illustration provided in chapter 3, "What do novice programmers think as they solve simple computer programs?" illustrates this type of SoTL question. "What is" questions focus on systematically analyzing and describing teaching and learning experiences. A third kind of question is "visions of the possible." This question leads to inquiry about what is most important. A fourth category of questions involves formulating a new conceptual framework for shaping thought about the practice of SoTL.

Craig Nelson (2003) provides a different framework for categorizing SoTL questions that tends to be organized around units of analysis. Nelson provided five different genres of SoTL:

1. *Reports of particular classes* include essays of "expert knowledge" about what worked. He includes both qualitative and quantitative before-and-after evaluations in this category.
2. *Reflection on several years of teaching, informed by other SoTL work* includes essays developing good ideas; summaries of expert knowledge gained by self-reflection and experimentation; and, perhaps most important, integration of larger frameworks into classroom and curriculum practice.
3. Nelson emphasizes that in his next category, *Larger Contexts: Comparison of Courses and Comparisons of Student Change Across Time,* he is referring to both qualitative and quantitative change.
4. *Learning Science* refers to the body of work that exists in human and animal learning. Most likely, your SoTL work will not fall into this category.
5. Last, since SoTL work should never occur in a vacuum, *Summaries and Analysis of Sets of Prior Studies* are critical as the field continues to progress.

Example Research Questions

Both Hutchings and Nelson provide a framework to help broaden your thinking about the particular question you would like to study. Begin by identifying what interests you in your own classroom or discipline or institution and reading some literature about your observation. Consider the situations that you simply do not understand or that you want to learn more about. SoTL work does not have to be abstract; it can involve asking real questions that are relevant to you personally. To illustrate, we explain several research questions that have motivated us in our SoTL work and include a few examples from other disciplines. The questions are varied, as were the studies that followed.

My research question arose naturally from my teaching experiences. I would think SoTL questions must occur every day to every teacher who is trying to perceive what students have learned, or why they aren't learning. In this case, over and over I saw my students failing to detect irony in a Kate Chopin short story where irony seemed quite plain to me in the text. I wanted to understand why, and what factors most influenced the likelihood that a student would perceive irony in the story. If I knew that, I would know more about where to concentrate my efforts in teaching them to read complex texts. —MARY JANE, ENGLISH

Effectiveness of a New Programming Language

As described in chapter 3, illustration 2, early in Cathy Bishop-Clark's career, she received permission to use a visual computer science programming language on a pilot basis to determine whether use of that language would help students better understand the fundamental concepts of computer programming. The computer language itself was new to the field and the department was reluctant to embrace such change without some evidence of its effectiveness. Throughout a 16-week semester, students in the pilot course used the visual rather than the text-based tool the rest of the department was using. The research theme in this case was "visual programming languages." The more specific question that arose from this theme was, "Do students using the visual programming language understand the fundamental concepts of computer programming better than those who are using the traditional text-based language?" (Bishop-Clark, 1998).

Effectiveness of Classroom Activities

In the early 2000s, we team-taught a course, titled "Psychology of the Internet," in which we developed several new classroom activities. The goal of the activities was to raise students' awareness of the psychological aspects of communicating in virtual environments. Our general theme in this case was "effectiveness of classroom activities" and our general research question was, "Are the classroom activities effective?" More specifically in this case we investigated four classroom activities. Our first specific research question was, "Was our activity in online friendship effective?" While each question was different (dropping in a different topic for each activity), our methods for investigating each question were the same (Dietz-Uhler & Bishop-Clark, 2002).

Abandoning the Lecture in Biology

In many science classes, such as introductory biology, large lectures are commonplace. Evans and Omaha Boy (1996) questioned whether there was a more effective way to use class time to facilitate learning. They speculated that students could learn more and be more satisfied with their biology experience if they learned using guided-learning activities and weekly exams. The general research theme Evans and Omaha Boy explored could be categorized as effectiveness of the lecture in science courses, whereas the specific question became whether it is more beneficial to student learning and student satisfaction to use guided learning activities rather than lectures in a biology class.

Improving In-Class Discussions

Like many professors, we struggle with in-class discussions. Sometimes, getting students engaged and motivated to discuss course topics is difficult. During the team-taught "Psychology of the Internet," we informally observed that class discussions that were preceded by virtual (online) chats seemed livelier and included more student participation. In an effort to improve the quantity and quality of in-class, face-to-face discussions, we began using virtual chats in the classroom. The online chat preceded the face-to-face discussion. Our research theme was "improving in-class discussions." The more specific question was, "Can the quality and quantity of in-class discussions be improved by a preceding online chat or a discussion board?" In this study, we became even more specific and stated the question in the form of a hypothesis. Our hypothesis was that "individuals who participated in computer-mediated conversation will have subsequent face-to-face discussions that are perceived to be more comfortable and offer a greater diversity of perspectives than face-to-face discussions not preceded by computer-mediated communications." We moved from a vague theme of how to improve in-class discussions to a very testable and specific research question. Admittedly, this question does not begin to get at the very complex nature of in-class discussions, but it does tease out one potential factor and allowed us to study one way to improve in-class discussions (Dietz-Uhler & Bishop-Clark, 2001).

Solving Programming Problems

As discussed in chapter 3, illustration 1, early in Cathy Bishop-Clark's teaching career she was having a difficult time understanding why so many students struggled with writing very simple computer programs. Solutions that were obvious to her and some of the stronger students were very frustrating to other students. She wanted an up-close and detailed picture of the students' minds as they worked through a program. In this case, her research theme was "novice programming." The specific research question was, "What do novice programmers think as they solve simple computer programs?" (Bishop-Clark, 1992).

In addition to the research questions we have identified, countless other studies investigate questions that fall into the SoTL category. Table 4.1 outlines several of these studies and lists the research question investigated in each of these studies. Notice that the questions vary in type, scope, and content.

Some questions are unique to the discipline; others have more of a cross-disciplinary focus. Some questions involve students in a single section of a classroom; others are broader in scope and include surveys of many different kinds of students. Many questions take years to answer, whereas other questions take only a term. In general the more specific and clear you can be when identifying your question, the better the subsequent study.

Literature Review

An essential part of all scholarly inquiry is to put the research question in the context of what has been done previously. SoTL work done in a vacuum does nothing to move the field as a whole forward. Once you have identified a research question, performing a literature review is an important next step. In addition to placing your work in the context of others', performing a complete literature review at this stage allows you to clarify and further revise your research question. If, for instance, you find that there are 100 studies in various disciplines using various groups of students that conclusively found that online chats do improve face-to-face discussions, there would be little point in performing yet another general study on the topic. However, that is rarely the case.

The idea for my research question came from replicating an idea from another study. I then added extension pieces to make the data richer. I also looked for priorities in my discipline and in my university and made sure the question I was going to investigate made sense from a lot of different levels. —BROOKE, NURSING

The research question guides your literature review. Begin by identifying key words or phrases. Identify both general and specific terms. Use a thesaurus and look for synonyms. Begin by exploring the work in your own discipline. Virtually all disciplines have a journal devoted to education. There is the *Journal of Computer Science Education*, the *Journal of Chemical Education, Teaching Psychology*, and the *Journal of Economic Education*, to name just a few. Appendix B includes a more complete list of pedagogical journals. These journals will give you a feel for the work done in your own discipline. By surveying this literature, you can begin to understand the most common methods used for SoTL work in your discipline. In addition to getting a feel for the methodologies used, you will learn what has been done in your own field with regard to your SoTL question. For instance, in the previous example in novice programming, the first step was to explore journals in computer science education to see what was known about novices learning to write computer programs. Not only did Cathy Bishop-Clark find specific articles on novice programming, she also found an entire edited collection on empirical investigations of novice programming.

The exploration of SoTL work does not end with a survey of the literature in your own field. Weimer (2006) makes a strong case for reviewing literature outside one's own field. She explains that SoTL work must be looked at broadly, and much can be learned from work outside the discipline. In fact, she explains that while her field is speech communication, she has learned the most from pedagogical periodicals in chemistry, engineering, management, sociology, and psychology. She explains several reasons for investigating literature outside your own discipline. First, when you go beyond your discipline, you enlarge and enrich your knowledge base. She explains that certain fields are more oriented toward certain methods. For instance, an engineering field is likely more quantitative in its exploration of pedagogical issues, while an English field may be more qualitative. When the question clearly crosses many disciplines, being familiar with methodological approaches from several different fields can greatly enhance your own study. In the novice programming examples, the literature from computer science education was largely quantitative. Many empirical studies gave glimpses into the mental models and processing of novice programming. None of the studies investigated at that time used qualitative methods. While reviewing studies in other areas comparing novice and expert knowledge, an example was found that was entirely qualitative. Using a protocol analysis, the students talked aloud as they solved a

TABLE 4.1
Example Research Questions

Author(s)	Question
Chizmar, 2005	1. Do assignments increase student learning when they (a) shift students' first exposure to new material from direct instruction during class time to their working independently outside class; and (b) use a time-efficient grading scheme? 2. Can assignments increase students' participation and learning when they (a) shift students' first exposure to new concepts from direct instruction during class time to their working independently outside class; and (b) use a time-efficient grading scheme?
Clark & Jones, 2001	1. How do online sections of a public-speaking course differ from traditional sections?
Clinton & Kohlmeyer, 2005	1. Will performance on the final exam be higher for students who took group quizzes than for those who did not take group quizzes? 2. Will students taking group quizzes earn higher student evaluations of teaching scores than students not taking group quizzes? 3. Will group quiz performance be better for groups that self-select their members than for individuals who are assigned to their groups by the instructor?
Denton, Adams, Blatt, & Lorish, 2000	1. Will including problem-based learning within a physical therapy graduate program be as effective in preparing graduates to perform essential job functions as a more traditional learning approach?
Finlay & Faulkner, 2005	1. Do reading groups encourage students to engage with a broader range of the literature? 2. Do reading groups encourage critical thinking around issues central to their subject area? 3. Do reading groups provide opportunities for active learning through peer learning and shared understandings?
Fleming, 2001	1. Does using a checklist, modified rubrics, and e-mail influence achievement and attitudes of students enrolled in a psychology class? 2. Will students who use a checklist outperform students who did not use a checklist on exam 1?
Hunt, Simonds, & Hinchliffe, 2000	1. Is using a student portfolio in a basic communication course an effective, authentic tool for course assessment?
O'Loughlin, 2002	1. Do interactive-learning activities in lecture stimulate more active student engagement in large science classes? 2. Do interactive-learning activities improve class performance measures, such as mean lecture-exam performance and final grades in large science classes?
Prehar, McCarthy, & Tucker, 2004	1. What factors underlie student intentions to participate in community service by applying the Theory of Planned Behavior? 2. What is the effectiveness of service-learning pedagogy for increasing students' willingness to participate in future community service?
Weckman & Scudder-Davis, 2005	1. Does teaching natural science to nonmajors with an individual instructor lead to different attitudes and cognitive changes than teaching with a team of experts?

problem. In this case the method chosen for the novice programmer study was identified only after looking at literature in disciplinary areas other than computer science.

I noticed in previous semesters that students were very intimidated to engage in peer review in foreign language. However, a couple of articles that I read before the project identified a positive contribution of peer review in foreign language writing. A combination of observing my students and reviewing some prior literature gave me the motivation to start the project. —EVA, SPANISH

A second benefit of a multidisciplinary literature search does not have to do with methods but instead with findings. When multiple disciplines report the same finding, that finding has much more power. In the illustration of the novice programmer, when we extended our search to novices versus experts, we learned that in many different fields, novices focused on superficial rather than deep characteristics. This had some strong implications and greatly informed our particular study on novice programmers. To make the most of what the SoTL body of work has to teach, we must approach the literature review with an open mind and be willing to explore work in fields other than our own. Such an approach allows us to expand our understanding of methodology and gives breadth to our interpretation of results.

In addition to looking at literature in different disciplines, we recommend that you look at the many journals devoted to college teaching and learning, which are interdisciplinary by their very nature. The *International Journal on the Scholarship of Teaching and Learning, College Teaching*, the *Journal of Excellence in College Teaching*, and *Teaching in Higher Education* are all cross-disciplinary journals with pedagogical content. Other journals are topic-based rather than discipline-based; *Active Learning in Higher Education, Journal of the First-Year Experience and Students in Transition*, and the *Journal of Student-Centered Learning* are just a few.

The resources you will use for SoTL work will be varied and may include journal articles, conference papers, dissertations, websites, government publications, theses and dissertations, and books. Be aware that when you restrict your attention to published research, you are likely to lose some unpublished, statistically insignificant findings. In cases where you can find little published work or the work is inconclusive, it may be worth tracking down the unpublished studies, dissertations, and technical reports. Much of the research done in higher education is never published.

Once you identify publications and begin to read the articles, it may be helpful to use tables or lists to systematically record the findings and the characteristics you review. It is useful to record the number of subjects, methodologies used, and characteristics of the environment. If groups were involved, pay attention to how the students were assigned to them. If pre- and post-tests were involved, pay attention to the instruments used for data collection and whether those instruments were reliable and valid. Note the extent of any effect.

How many studies you review depends on many factors. Clearly, most faculty members do not have the resources or time to review every piece of literature that has been published related to a particular research question, especially given the interdisciplinary nature of SoTL work. You should review the literature until you feel comfortable that you have a representative sample of the body of work that exists in your field. In the novice programmer example, when Cathy Bishop-Clark identified the edited collection of works specifically related to novice programming and reviewed some of the general literature on novice and expert processing, she felt like she had a "representative sample."

The final step of your literature review is to analyze and interpret the reviewed work. Recall that one of the primary reasons for a literature review is to better inform your question. As you review the literature, can you make generalizations? Could the methods used have created conflicts? What are the strengths and weaknesses of prior studies? Did you learn that your question has been answered conclusively and additional work in this area is not likely to be of benefit?

Involving Students

At our campus, we frequently have formal student/faculty dialogues in which we meet off-campus for dinner. In these dialogues, we always learn a tremendous amount about our students' perceptions of teaching and learning. We listen to students discuss how they view their classes, other students, and their professors. Similarly, as a formative evaluation, faculty often incorporate a small-group instructional diagnosis (SGID) into their classroom. This classroom evaluation technique involves having a third party solicit information from the students, including what is going well, what is not going well, and ideas to improve the course. The SGIDs are completed in the middle of a term so that the instructor can use that information to improve the class and/or talk with the students about the feedback. It has been our experience that both of these events (the formal student/faculty dialogues and the SGID) lead to a wealth of research questions. Simply talking with students generates many interesting ideas, including questions the students themselves may be interested in researching.

Involving the students in your review of the literature may be a straightforward path to involvement; one can simply hire students to identify relevant literature. But in some classes, it may be relevant for the students to identify a research question. The students, along with the faculty member, could then each review several pieces of related work. In a class of 25 students, you may instantly have 25 different pieces of related work. Students and faculty can then work together to see how that literature informs or modifies the question.

Generating Your Research Idea Worksheet

The first step in your SoTL investigation is to identify the research question. The importance of this step cannot be overemphasized. The research question defines every aspect of your study—how many people you will study, the literature you will review, the research techniques and methods available to you, the techniques used for data collection, etc. The clearer and more precise your question, the more likely you are to have a successful study. To help you move from a general research theme to a well-defined, clear research question, we have outlined a series of questions. Note that we have given you only a small area in which to write each question. This is intentional.

Identify your research theme, the general area you would like to investigate. Be sure to write in the form of a question.

Identify your research question. Based on this theme, can you identify several more specific research questions? Be sure to write in the form of a question.

Identify a "too-specific" research question. Next, write your question, getting even more specific and reducing your question to an even smaller unit. Write each of your question(s) on a smaller scale, in terms as precise as possible. Be sure to write in the form of a question.

Identify the question(s) that make the most sense to you and have your colleagues review the question(s). Review your three questions and write the question that is at the level that makes the most sense to you.

Identify key words. Once you have identified your research question, you will need to review the literature related to the question you wish to investigate. Begin by identifying the key words that will help you locate the literature that may be relevant to your particular study. Consider both broad and narrow key words.

Broad Key Words	Specific Key Words

Consider resources. Identify specific journals or indexes you plan on searching during your literature review.

Discipline-Specific	General SoTL Publications

Identify three resources. Based on the items you have defined, review three publications related to your SoTL project. As you review the articles, pay attention to details such as who was studied, how they were studied, and what measures were used. See if there are themes related to this work. Fill out the table as you identify how the resources relate to your study.

Title/Author	Description of the Study	How It Relates to Your Study

Interpret your findings. Are the methods used in prior work the same as or different from yours? Will your work build on work that already exists?

How will your research be the same as previous work?	How will your research be different from previous work?

Revise your question. In the space provided identify your revised research question, which may have changed as a result of the literature review.

Generating Your Research Idea: Completed Worksheet

Identify your research theme, the general area you would like to investigate. Be sure to write in the form of a question.

> Does using the Alice programming language have any impact on teaching beginning programmers?

Identify your research question. Based on this theme, can you identify several more specific research questions? Be sure to write in the form of a question.

> Will students improve their understanding of computer programming if they use Alice?

Identify a "too-specific" research question. Next, write your question, getting even more specific and reducing your question to an even smaller unit. Write each of your question(s) on a smaller scale, in terms as precise as possible. Be sure to write in the form of a question.

> Will student scores on a confidence test improve after a single class session using Alice?
>
> Will student scores on an enjoyment test improve after a single class session using Alice?
>
> Will student scores on understanding one aspect of programming improve after a single class session using Alice?

Identify the question(s) that make the most sense to you and have your colleagues review the question(s). Review your three questions and write the question that is at the level that makes the most sense to you.

> Will students increase their confidence in programming after a 2.5-week session using Alice?
>
> Will students increase their enjoyment of programming after a 2.5-week session using Alice?
>
> Will students improve their knowledge of programming after a 2.5-week session using Alice?

Identify key words. Once you have identified your research question, you will need to review the literature related to the question you wish to investigate. Begin by identifying the key words that will help you locate the literature that may be relevant to your particular study. Consider both broad and narrow key words.

Broad Key Words	Specific Key Words
Novice programming	Alice programming
Confidence	Objects-first programming language
Attitudes	Alice & confidence
Liberal education courses	Alice & attitudes

Consider resources. Identify specific journals or indexes you plan on searching during your literature review.

Discipline-Specific	General SoTL Publications

Journal of Educational Computing Research
    Proceedings of SIGCSE (Special Interest
    Group Computer Science Education)
Communications of the ACM
Proceedings of International Conference on
    Software Engineering
	International Journal of Scholarship of
	    Teaching and Learning
	College Teaching
	Journal of Excellence in College Teaching
	Active Learning in Higher Education

Identify three resources. Based on the items you have defined, review three publications related to your SoTL project. As you review the articles, pay attention to details such as who was studied, how they were studied, and what measures were used. See if there are themes related to this work. Fill out the table as you identify how the resources relate to your study.

Title/Author	Description of the Study	How It Relates to Your Study
Cooper, S., Dann, W., & Pausch, R. (2003). Teaching objects-first in introductory computer science. *Proceedings of the 34th SIGCSE technical symposium on computer science education*, Reno, Nevada.	Forty-nine students taking a first programming course were invited to take the Alice programming course. The mean results for student who had used Alice were 2.8, compared to 1.3 for the students who did not take the Alice course. All students were at risk.	Like our study, this study investigates whether students who use Alice increase in performance in content knowledge.
Moskel, B., Lurie, D., & Cooper, S. (2004). Evaluating the effectiveness of a new instructional approach. *Proceedings of the 35th SIGCSE technical symposium on computer science education* (pp. 75–79).	This study investigated student performance, retention, attitudes, and confidence after using Alice for either half or all of a semester.	This study investigates very similar constructs (performance, attitude, and confidence).
Kelleher, C., & Pausch, R. (2005). Lowering the barriers to programming: A taxonomy of programming environments and languages for novice programmers. *ACM Computing Surveys, 37*(2), 83–137.	Provides a summary of programming environments that have been designed to facilitate learning computer programming. From the text-based languages of the 1960s to the graphics-based environments of today, there is little consensus on how to facilitate the process of learning computer programming.	This piece is not directly related to Alice programming but provides an excellent context for the study by reviewing similar work of the last 40 years.

Interpret your findings. Are the methods used in prior work the same as or different from yours? Will your work build on work that already exists?

How will your research be the same as previous work?	How will your research be different from previous work?
One study indicates that using Alice increased retention and increased grades. Our study will look at programming performance. One study indicates no improvement in attitude after using Alice. Our study will also study whether there is an improvement in attitude. Other educators have used Alice to prepare students for introductory computer science courses. We are also using Alice with introductory computing students.	Because the language is so new, we identified only a handful of studies that investigated Alice programming. All of the studies identified were 100% quantitative. Our work will include both a qualitative and quantitative picture of using Alice with novice programmers.

Revise your question. In the space provided identify your revised research question, which may have changed as a result of the literature review.

In this case, the questions remained the same. Will student increase their confidence in programming after a 2.5-week session using Alice? Will students increase their enjoyment of programming after a 2.5-week session using Alice? Will students improve their knowledge of programming after a 2.5-week session using Alice?

Designing the Study

5

ONCE YOU HAVE clearly identified a SoTL research question, your next step is to figure out the best way to answer that question. Your question defines every aspect of your study—especially the study design. Many different kinds of SoTL designs can be used, ranging from interviewing a single student to an experiment involving hundreds of students. Each of these design approaches can provide valuable and important information about how our students learn. The goal of this chapter is to help you identify the best design approaches to answer your particular SoTL research question.

In the following sections we first discuss, in very broad terms, the difference between quantitative and qualitative methods. We discuss the value of pilot studies and encourage you to think of your SoTL work as a series of investigations rather than as a single study at one time. We move to discussing whom you want to study, how long, and how many, and then briefly discuss the use of comparison groups. Last, we describe various research approaches: descriptive, case, observation, interviews, focus groups, survey, experimental, and quasi-experimental. Each of these approaches can help provide answers to the SoTL question you are asking.

I was anxious about whether or not my study was going to tell me results that could be meaningful to my profession. I was very concerned that the study would become bigger than life and consume all of my time in order to get something out of it. —DEBBIE, NURSING

Quantitative, Qualitative, or Both?

There are two general categories of research designs: quantitative and qualitative. If your SoTL question needs to have some kind of numerical evaluation, then at least part of your data collection will be quantitative. SoTL questions such as whether one group does better than another or whether a teaching technique results in improved learning are likely to use a quantitative design. Quantitative designs tend to follow a similar process: make a prediction or hypothesis, collect data, analyze data, and draw conclusions. For example, a quantitative study attempting to evaluate students' ability to apply complex reasoning skills when solving a problem may include an evaluation instrument that all students in the class take. The instrument may present a series of problems the student is asked to solve, each requiring the student to apply the complex reasoning skill learned. Or, if the situation allows, the quantitative researcher may divide the students randomly into two different breakout groups. One group may learn the skill of interest using a hands-on experiment; the other group may learn the skill using a peer tutor. Learning in both groups might be assessed using the same evaluation instrument.

These evaluations can be compared using statistical analysis and the researcher can draw conclusions based on this analysis.

If your data incorporate verbal, visual, or textual information, you probably will have to draw on qualitative methods. Questions such as "How does a student learn?" or "What is a student thinking as he or she solves a complex problem?" tend to require a qualitative approach. For a qualitative study attempting to understand students' ability to apply complex reasoning skills, the researcher would study students' participation in the natural setting, perhaps becoming a student of the class and observing what happens. Or the researcher may conduct an in-depth interview with each student or get a small group of students together for a conversation about why they solved problems in the way that they did. Qualitative research tends to be less structured and includes observation, and data collected in more spontaneous and open-ended ways.

Your SoTL research question will point you in a direction that tends to be either qualitative or quantitative and your discipline is likely to partly define your question. In a highly quantitative field such as mathematics or engineering, your SoTL work may be more likely to be accepted and valued if you follow the norms of the field. Your own personal style plays a role in the direction you choose. Some of us tend to view the world in terms of quantitative changes. We are interested in whether the mean exam score improves as a result of using a particular teaching technique. Other SoTL researchers would be very frustrated to simplify an environment as rich and complex as the teaching environment to a series of numbers.

Quantitative and qualitative designs each answer different kinds of questions. Questions that are stated in forms such as, "Has there been an increase?" "Did one group perform better than another?" and "Did a teaching method lead to increased scores?" are likely to be quantitative. Questions that involve more explanation such as, "Why did students dislike the study of . . . ?" or "How did students understand?" are more likely to be qualitative.

While the debate about the comparative merits of qualitative and quantitative methods continues to rage in the academic community, it is increasingly the case that the value and strengths of each method are being acknowledged. Research that combines both qualitative and quantitative techniques is growing in impor-

tance and is referred to as "mixed method." Mixed method research combines the strengths of both quantitative and qualitative designs. A mixed method approach may include both random assignment and counts of times participated, but it may also include interviews with students, giving some insight into the very complex nature of classroom participation.

I used both qualitative and quantitative data to answer my research question. It served my purposes best, using the qualitative to explain the quantitative. I had the numbers and some explanation as to what was driving those numbers. —MICHELLE, PSYCHOLOGY

Pilot Studies

As you identify and plan your SoTL project, you should think carefully about a variety of issues: your research question, whom you will study, what you expect your outcomes to be, what types of methods you will use, and what kind of instruments you will use. Careful planning of design will help ensure a successful project; however, actually doing the research almost always presents unforeseen challenges or opportunities. A pilot study is a study typically done on a small scale to help you identify some of those unforeseen challenges or opportunities. Light and colleagues (1990) explain that there are three specific kinds of pilot studies that are particularly useful: (1) a pilot in which new instruments are designed, (2) a pilot that will shape a future experiment, and (3) a pilot that is a small-scale version of a future experiment. While these authors focus primarily on a certain kind of design (experimental), the framework they create works for many different SoTL designs. We maintain that pilot studies are almost always worth the time and effort they require. No design is so complete that it can't be improved by a pilot study. Such studies can last an hour, a day, a week, or a semester.

It is important to think of a project in terms of phases. Indeed, much of our SoTL work has involved a multiphase approach, with the pilot study being the first phase. For instance, in 2005, Cathy Bishop-Clark began investigating whether the use of a new programming language would be an effective way to teach. At first, she started with a study that lasted only two class sessions. This small-scale study helped her understand a variety of issues that we did not foresee and narrow and further define the instrument she used to measure content understanding. She learned that a few of the questions used on the original instrument did not measure what she thought they would. Based on this preliminary study, she dropped several questions from the survey and realized that one of the exercises we were using was far too long to be completed in a single class session as originally planned. The bottom line is that by trying out her SoTL project on a small scale, Cathy learned much about implementing her project the following semester on a much larger scale (multiple sections, two weeks).

Not only did the pilot study have a strong influence on the full-blown study, but in this case the results of the pilot study were published (Bishop-Clark, Courte, & Howard, 2006). The results of the large-scale, full-blown SoTL project were published a year later (Bishop-Clark, Courte, Evans, & Howard, 2007). As you design your own SoTL project, think in terms of phases. Start small—very small—and move incrementally to larger-scale projects. Occasionally, the pilot study is of such quality that it can be presented or published.

Phasing my SoTL research allows me to develop and share a deeper understanding of service learning, which directly impacts the quality of my teaching, service, and scholarship. I am studying many different aspects and layers of the same subject; in small pieces, in larger pieces, over time, and with different compounding variables, which keeps it interesting. However, since I am always focused on my basic interest and practice of service learning, I feel like I've been able to center myself and work smarter, rather than spinning in circles.
—BROOKE, NURSING

Who, How Long, and How Many?

Who? The Student you study depends on your research question and how generalizable you would like your work to be. In some of the research we have done, our work has focused primarily on a specific group. For instance, some of Cathy's work has in-

volved novice computer programmers. The students she studied were beginning programming students and most were computer science majors. The generalizability of the results was very limited. On the other hand, in another study, we were interested in the impact of an online chat on subsequent face-to-face discussions. In this case the students we studied were enrolled in a university-required course. Students represented a variety of majors and came from three different campuses of the same institution. The second study clearly is more generalizable than the first, but even the second is limited. In the second we still collected data from students in a single institution (although they represented three different campuses), and the majority of the students we studied were freshmen or sophomores. The broader and more representative your sample, the more generalizable your results.

How long? Your time frame may be a single class session, a several-week unit, an entire semester, or even a long-term or longitudinal study, which involves keeping track of a student after he or she has graduated from your class or program. One of our recurring themes when teaching others how to do SoTL work is "Keep it simple!" Your first SoTL study does not need to be a longitudinal study that follows students from their college days to their adult lives, for example. Begin small and design subsequent studies that build on your first study and become larger in scope and generalizability. Depending on your research question, it may be completely appropriate for your first SoTL study to be a single class session.

How many? Like "who" and "how long," the question of "how many" again depends on the research question. Many factors define how many, including the type of method you choose. In general, if you are doing qualitative research, a single small group or a limited number of students may be appropriate. However, if your data are quantitative in nature, generally the more students you can involve, the better and more powerful your results. While you may be limited by your class size, it sometimes makes sense to include students outside your particular sections. For instance, if you are teaching an introductory English course and your time frame is only a single class session, consider investigating whether your English colleagues would be willing to allow you to teach one of their class sessions, which would enable you to collect far more data.

*I asked my English colleagues to gather data for me because I knew that I needed a large sample and that I needed student papers from students **who were not my students** in order to eliminate at least one variable (teaching to the prompt). I sent around a request to the entire teaching faculty asking them to administer two separate essays. I gave them enough advance warning that they were able to build the two assignments into their syllabi; I believe that I would never have gotten so much cooperation if I hadn't been able to work so far in advance.* —KELLI, ENGLISH

Comparison Groups

Consider whether a comparison group makes sense for your SoTL project. To illustrate, consider a study in which we investigated whether students who participated in an online chat experience had better subsequent face-to-face discussions. We could have studied a single group that first engaged in online chat before a face-to-face discussion, and we could have measured how they felt about their discussion. We could have come to some conclusions based on our findings. However, our findings became far more powerful when we added a group that did not have an online chat before holding a classroom discussion on the same topic. In this case, it wasn't necessary for both to discuss the same topic. The group that didn't have a chat session was our control group. The results of the two-group study are clearly the more reliable and more convincing of the two designs. Of course, as with any SoTL work, many practical issues must be considered.

Since I had the good fortune of teaching two sections of the same course, I was able to modify a variable to compare the outcomes. Determining which variable to modify was the hard part, but with mentoring from the faculty learning community's leaders and the participants, I was able to find a solution. I changed the timing of a quiz in the presentation of a special topical study. —JENNIFER, ART HISTORY

Research Approach

This section of the chapter describes various research approaches you can use to answer your research question: descriptive, case, observation, interviews, focus groups, survey, experimental, and quasi-experimental. Each approach requires a different set of knowledge and skills. Some will be more accepted in your disciplinary field, and some may appeal to you more than others. Select the approach or set of approaches that best answers your particular question, that is most appropriate in your field, and that motivates you.

As we looked at various ways to do SoTL research, I was able to imagine my study through the lens of each approach. Some would clearly offer results and others not, dependent on the research question I had identified. I also knew that I needed to find a way to get data—numbers, even—from writing samples, which required a particular approach to the work. —KELLI, ENGLISH

Studying teaching and learning is incredibly interesting, complex, multifaceted, and difficult. An attitude survey cannot begin to enable us to understand the rich relationship between attitudes and learning. An in-depth interview with a single person provides a glimpse into such depth, but it is only a glimpse into the perceptions of a single person. Each of the methods we describe has both strengths and limitations. None of the methods provides a comprehensive view of teaching and learning, but each provides us with an approach to understand the teaching and learning environment in a different way.

Descriptive

A descriptive SoTL research design does exactly what the title implies—that is, it describes a current situation or paints a picture. Descriptive research does not test predictions nor does it imply any cause-and-effect relationships. The U.S. Census is an example of descriptive research: it surveys and describes a current population of the United States at one point in time. Descriptive SoTL projects answer questions such as, "How well do students solve mathematics problems?" "How do students perform on final exams in psychology at my institution?" or "What are the study patterns for students preparing for a recent quiz?" Descriptive data can be collected in a variety of ways. Surveys, interviews, focus groups, and case studies are all different ways of describing the current state of affairs.

Online course management systems provide a repository of data that can also be categorized as descriptive. From a course management system you can see how often students access the content, what time of day they access material, and how long they take to complete a quiz. You can also view quiz, test, and course averages. You can view the high grade, low grade, and distribution of grades. All of this gives you a kind of snapshot of certain aspects of your course.

One of the most personally informative SoTL studies Cathy published (Bishop-Clark, 2006) was a SoTL project in which she simply described a service-learning project and student attitudes about that project. In this course, students were required to design a web-based computer system for an elementary school teacher. While learning the theory of systems design, students designed computer systems for second- and third-grade students to use. Descriptions were based on observations, exam questions related to the project, a questionnaire for the elementary school teacher, and observation of class participation. The objective of this particular SoTL project was to describe in a complete and systematic way what was observed, what Cathy's students reported, what the elementary school teacher observed, and how Cathy's students reacted. Similarly, Evans and Omaha Boy (1996) describe the results of a two-year pilot study of a one-semester biology course for non-science students. As with the Bishop-Clark study, the authors describe students' exam grades, class averages, and overall satisfaction in a course that did not use a single lecture. Both papers were written so that other teachers of the same course could understand reactions to the project and replicate learning similar projects in their own courses.

Descriptive research projects allow us to observe natural situations without affecting them—just as in the previous two studies that carefully described a learning situation without attempting to influence it in any way. Descriptive research methods are not without weaknesses. With descriptive research we cannot suggest any causal relationship. For instance, we could not conclude that students learned more because of the service-learning project, or that replacing the lecture improved the outcomes of the biology class. Descriptive research is often a precursor to additional studies, but occasionally a descriptive SoTL project can stand alone.

Descriptive projects have a powerful place in SoTL work. The ultimate goal of SoTL work is to improve teaching and learning. By describing our innovative teaching and student reactions to that teaching in a systematic and careful way, we help ensure that such techniques are applied beyond our own classroom. Table 5.1 provides additional resources for descriptive projects.

Case Study

A case study is a methodology that describes in detail a specific event, person, or group. The researcher observes the environment, investigates archival documents, and interviews various members of the community. Some case studies involve long-term investigations. For instance, one case study may investigate a single person's educational goals and how they relate to that individual's accomplishments as an adult. One basic premise of case study research is to study the event or person within the natural environment as much as possible. While some kinds of research involve controlling the environment, the case study focuses on just the opposite. In short, a case study is a form of descriptive research focusing on a sample of

TABLE 5.1 Descriptive Resources		
Book	*Sample SoTL Study by Authors*	*Sample SoTL Study by Others*
Salkind, N. J. (2006). *Exploring research* (chap. 9). Upper Saddle River, NJ: Pearson.	Bishop-Clark, C. (2006). Problem-based service learning in a 200-level systems analysis and design course. *Information Systems Education Journal, 4*(100).	Evans, R. C., & Omaha Boy, N. H. (1996). Abandoning the lecture in biology. *Journal on Excellence in College Teaching, 7*(3), 93–110.

one: one community, one person, one classroom, one assignment, or one quiz.

Marcia Baxter Magolda (2001) undertook a longitudinal study of college students. She followed them from their undergraduate days until their early 30s to understand how they made meaning of their lives and how their college education influenced that meaning making. Her work was based on case studies of individual students. She looked at each student individually and interviewed each one many times over a period of years. Based on this very rich and complex data set, Magolda makes recommendations about how to revitalize and reframe higher education.

Clearly, Magolda's work has profound implications and it is considered classic. But not all SoTL case studies need to be of this scale. Several of the SoTL studies the authors have published can be considered case studies. In a 2003 study (Bishop-Clark & Dietz-Uhler, 2003), we describe an innovative classroom activity and student reactions to that activity. We essentially studied a single assignment. In this assignment, we asked students to communicate electronically for about a week with several different individuals whom they had not met and did not know. The students communicated with these individuals using only the discussion boards and online chats. During a face-to-face classroom session, we talked as a class about our impressions of these individuals based on our electronic conversations. We discussed whether we felt the individual was male or female, short or tall, abled or disabled. Then we actually met the individuals with whom we had communicated electronically. We compared the impressions we had electronically with the impressions we made in a face-to-face setting and spent time exploring the psychological concepts at work. We learned that these students were highly motivated and very much enjoyed this kind of activity.

While many SoTL projects involve hundreds of students, as we already stated, the work involved in a case study has a sample size, or *n*, of one—whether it be one classroom or one student. However, the work involved in something as simple as an investigation of a single student processing a single assignment can be substantial and complex. In addition to being very time-consuming, it may be difficult if not impossible to remain objective if the case study is of *your* assignment or one of *your* students, given that you will have such a vested interest in the outcome. Another drawback of case studies is that since they study a single situation, like other forms of descriptive research, they are not generalizable to other settings. However, since learning is an incredibly complex activity, case studies can provide rich and descriptive evaluations of teaching and learning. Table 5.2 provides additional resources for case study projects.

Observation

Observational methods allow you to gather firsthand information on an educational process or technique. As educators we are already acute observers of what happens in our classroom. We notice students' body language, their eyes, and their participation. And we regularly use this information to evaluate learning and attitudes. A student whose eyes light up during a learning activity projects a very different message from the student who is nodding off.

By observing a situation and its surroundings, we can develop a more holistic picture of the impact of our teaching and better understand the context of the learning environment. Observational approaches allow us to learn things about students that they may be unwilling or unable to express. They may further validate the attitudes students report in a survey or observations may highlight discrepancies. Furthermore, observations can provide good opportunities for identifying unanticipated outcomes.

While we may already use observations regularly, using observational methods as a research approach is

TABLE 5.2 Case Study Resources		
Book	*Sample SoTL Study by Authors*	*Sample SoTL Study by Others*
Yin, R. K. (2008). *Case study research: Design and methods.* Newbury Park, CA: Sage.	Bishop-Clark, C., & Dietz-Uhler, B. (2003). Forming online impressions: A class exercise. *Journal of Educational Technology Systems, 31*(3), 251–260.	Saunders, M. D. (1998). The service learner as researcher: A case study. *Journal on Excellence in College Teaching, 9*(2), 55–67.

more formal. Ideally, the observer is a highly trained participant who blends into the environment (like a fly on the wall). The extent of participation varies and depends on the role the observer takes. It is important that the observer does not change the situation in any way. When the president of the university sits in on a particular class, and the students know the observer is the president, students are very likely to change their behavior. When we are using observation as a research methodology, we want students to behave as they normally do. Observers can record the setting, the social environment, the implementation of activities, the nonverbal communications, and the verbal communications. Observers can count the number of questions asked and rank both the type and quality of those questions. Ideally, the observer should not be the educator or the researcher.

Visioli, Lodi, Carrassi, and Zannini (2009) used observation to explore how teachers exhibit desirable lecturing skills. They observed how lecturing skills affected students' attention. In this study the authors prepared an "observational grid" divided into four categories: explaining, questioning, visual aids, and lecturer attitude. A third party observed and recorded observations. The authors analyzed those observations and concluded that the lecturer's attitude appeared to have the most impact on student attention. In this example, observational research was used to stimulate reflection among the lecturers and to improve the lecturing skills of the faculty members involved in the study. Table 5.3 provides additional resources for observation-type projects.

Interviews

Interviews are perhaps the most common form of qualitative research method. Interviews allow the interviewer to understand in a detailed way the perspectives of participants. The primary task of the interview is to understand the meaning of what the interviewees say (Kvale, 1996). Interviews allow us to understand perspectives in much different ways from how survey research does.

There are several kinds of interviews, including conversational interviews, structured interviews, and in-depth interviews. Conversational interviews are informal with no predetermined questions. Such conversations may simply occur in hallways, after class, without preplanning. While such conversations are not planned, they may lead to valuable insight into a particular course or student learning. Structured interviews are exactly as they sound. All interviewees are asked the same questions and are asked to choose answers from a predetermined set of alternatives. The data collected with a structured interview can be very similar to what is collected in a survey.

In-depth or semistructured interviews sit between the conversational interview and the structured interview. They allow us to collect information in a detailed and more flexible way. Patton (1987) gives examples of questions for which the in-depth interview is especially useful. We have modified these questions slightly so they illustrate examples relevant for a SoTL project focused on online learning.

- What changes do you perceive in yourself as a result of participating in the online course?
- What features of the online course were most important to your learning?
- What did you expect you would learn when the course began?

TABLE 5.3 Observation Resources		
Book	*Sample SoTL Study by Authors*	*Sample SoTL Studies by Others*
Frechtling, J., & Sharp, L. (Eds.). (1997). *User-friendly handbook for mixed method evaluations* (chap. 3). Arlington, VA: National Science Foundation.	Bishop-Clark, C. (1992). Protocol analysis of a novice programmer. *SIGSCE Bulletin, 24*(3), 14–18.	Considine, J. R., Meyers, R. A., & Timerman, C. E. (2006). Evidence use in group quiz discussions: How do students support preferred choices? *Journal on Excellence in College Teaching, 17*(3), 65–89; Treisman, P. U. (1990). Studying students studying calculus: A look at the lives of minority mathematics students in college. *The College Mathematics Journal, 23*(5), 362–372.

- What did you expect of an online course when the course began?
- Do you have experience taking online courses?
- What did you know about online learning prior to taking the course, and what do you know about online learning now?

In-depth interviews allow extensive probing of open-ended questions. They are far more personal than a survey and are especially appropriate when the research question is complex and detailed. In-depth interviews are also very appropriate when the data are sensitive. Often the data yielded from an in-depth interview provide new insights and reveal details that might not surface otherwise. For instance, rather than asking students to simply state the number of hours they studied for a particular course, we can ask why the students studied so often or so seldom.

Randall, Buschner, and Swerkes (1995) provide an excellent example of using interviews to understand the systematic differences among the learning style preferences of physical education majors. A total of 70 students were interviewed for approximately 30 minutes each. They were asked questions like, "What kind of teaching style or classroom environment motivates you to learn?" and "What can professors do to help you learn?" These interviews were audiotaped and transcribed into about 400 pages of verbatim text. The authors then analyzed the text to identify the major theoretical constructs or common themes. Once they had identified common themes, the authors used a method of constant comparison to put data into categories. Software allowed the researchers to code, recode, and sort data, and the authors identified patterns based on the analysis of the interview data.

Like all of the methods outlined in this section, interviewing requires practice and training. The interviewer needs to be sure to identify an appropriate setting for the interview (private, distraction-free, non-threatening) and create an environment in which the interviewee feels comfortable engaging and elaborating. The interviewer must take care not to slant either the questions or the way he or she interprets the responses. Perhaps the most important skill is the ability to listen carefully. The interviewer may choose to record the interview or simply take notes. Table 5.4 provides additional resources for projects involving interviews.

Focus Groups

Conducting focus groups is a qualitative methodology in which small groups of people are asked questions about their perceptions, beliefs, and attitudes. Focus groups are similar to interviews, but they involve people interacting with one another. They have the same objective as an interview: to draw out relevant and sometimes detailed information about the topic of interest. A typical focus group involves a small number of participants (fewer than 10), occurs during a brief period of time (30–60 minutes), and involves a moderator or facilitator. Ideally, the moderator should not be involved in the study, but should be a neutral third party. The participants are encouraged to speak freely. The moderator's job is to generate conversations about the topic of interest and keep those conversations focused on the topic. Typically, one student comment motivates other comments and a deeper conversation ensues. Focus groups tend to be lively and promote discussion.

We have used focus groups in several of our SoTL studies. In our case, we used focus groups in addition to another technique such as a survey or experiment. As an educator, it is extremely useful to hear students talking firsthand about a topic related to teaching and

TABLE 5.4	
Interview Resources	
Book	*Sample SoTL Studies by Others*
Weiss, R. S. (1994). *Learning from strangers— The art and method of qualitative interview studies.* New York: The Free Press.	Randall, L. E., Buschner, C., & Swerkes, B. (1995). Learning style preferences of physical education majors: Implications for teaching and learning. *Journal on Excellence in College Teaching, 6*(2), 57–77; Saunders, G., & Klemming, F. (2003). Integrating technology into a traditional learning environment: Reasons for and risks of success. *Active Learning in Higher Education, 4*(1), 74–86.

learning. For instance, in our study of using Alice (Bishop-Clark et al., 2007), we held several focus groups with the students who tried this new approach to computer programming. We took care to be sure that the teacher of the course was not the moderator of the focus group. Through the focus groups, we learned what students found particularly frustrating, their misconceptions, and what especially motivated them. The conversation in the focus group provided a level of depth that the survey and quiz could not.

Randall and DeCastron-Ambrosetti (2009) provide another example of using focus groups in SoTL research. Like our study, they used a combination of qualitative and quantitative techniques. They analyzed the impact of using literature circles in a university classroom. The goal of the study was to gain a broad perspective on the ways students attach meaning to the disciplinary literature and to better understand the role of the literature circles in the study of adolescence. The 31 participants were divided into groups of three to five students each and were asked:

1. What was your overall reaction to the literature circle?
2. How did your participation in the group lead to "shared meaning"?
3. What strong feelings or insights resulted from your participation in the literature circle?
4. What unique background, knowledge, or experience did you bring to the group?

Focus group sessions were video- and audiotaped, then the audiotapes were transcribed and analyzed to identify theoretical categories. Once themes were identified, interview data units were sorted into categories using the method of constant comparison. HyperRESEARCH (computer software) was used to code responses into the four themes. The researcher then interpreted and modified the emerging categories.

Berg (2007) provides excellent detail on the advantages and disadvantages of conducting focus groups. On the plus side, Berg points out that focus groups are highly flexible and are especially well-suited for certain audiences, such as those that are more transient, as in the case of students who are in a single-semester course and then move on. Focus groups allow for gathering large amounts of information in a short time and provide insight into how participants come to certain conclusions. It is one thing to have a group of students "strongly agree" that a certain teaching technique was effective, but it is entirely different to listen to students explain why that technique was so effective. Focus groups can provide insights into topics that are not well understood and can allow the moderator to explore unanticipated topics that arise during a group's discussion.

Conducting focus groups also has disadvantages. The success of the focus group and the quality of the data are deeply influenced by the moderator, and the moderator's expectations can greatly influence the direction of the conversation. Focus group attendance is typically voluntary and sometimes attracts the students with common characteristics. Only group, not individual, opinions are obtained, and as with any group, sometimes the dominant personality prevails. While focus groups can provide detail that a survey cannot, Berg (2007) points out that the data collected in focus groups are not as rich as data collected in an in-depth interview or through weeks of observation. Table 5.5

TABLE 5.5		
Focus Group Resources		
Books	*Sample SoTL Study by Authors*	*Sample SoTL Study by Others*
Krueger, R. A., & Casey, M. A. (2000). *Focus groups: A practical guide for applied research.* Thousand Oaks, CA: Sage; Stewart, D. W., & Shamdasani, P. N. (1990) *Focus groups: Theory and practice.* Thousand Oaks, CA: Sage.	Bishop-Clark, C., Courte, J., Evans, D., & Howard, E. (2007). A quantitative and qualitative investigation of using Alice programming to improve confidence, enjoyment and achievement among non-majors. *Journal of Educational Computing Research, 37*(2), 193–207.	Randall, L. E., & DeCastro-Ambrosetti, D. (2009). Analysis of student responses to participation in literature circles in a university classroom. *Journal on Excellence in College Teaching, 20*(2), 69–103.

provides additional resources for projects involving focus groups.

Surveys

Interview and focus group research are both considered forms of survey research. With the interview, you have a more in-depth conversation with a single student. With focus groups, you still are able to delve in depth but the emphasis is on a small group. Surveys in the form of questionnaires allow you to question hundreds, if not thousands, of students. Like all of the other methods we describe in this section, ample literature exists on how to develop, design, sample, and administer surveys, and on the theory and procedures involved.

We are all familiar with at least one type of survey: the end-of-term student evaluation of you and your class. We can use this information to affirm our effectiveness as educators or to modify the way we teach the course in subsequent terms. Surveys used in SoTL research are used for the same reasons.

Surveys can take a variety of forms. They can be administered via paper and pencil through the mail, paper and pencil in the classroom, e-mail, the web, and telephone. We have used some form of surveys in most of the SoTL work we have done. Lynch and Bishop-Clark (1993) conducted a series of studies with both traditional and nontraditional students on their attitudes toward learning in the classroom. In this situation, we telephone-interviewed students. In a different study (Bishop-Clark et al., 2007) we used a web-based questionnaire to get to two important dimensions of the classroom: learning and attitudes. While in the classroom, students completed the web-based questionnaire. In other instances, when computers were not readily available, we surveyed students with the old-fashioned paper-and-pencil questionnaire (Dietz-Uhler & Bishop-Clark, 2001).

Denton, Adams, Blatt, and Lorish (2000) describe a study that used surveys with two groups: students and employers. These authors studied whether using problem-based learning changed graduate performance outcomes in a physical therapy program. They compared learning outcomes of a group whose members experienced the curriculum in the form of problem-based learning with outcomes of a group whose members experienced the curriculum without it. Surveys were administered to employers and students. Student perceptions of the problem-based learning

approach were obtained from course and curriculum evaluations. Employer perceptions were measured by a survey that employers completed based on observing graduates' performances. More specifically, the survey assessed employers' perceptions of the graduates' job performance in professional behavior and management, problem solving, and patient evaluation and treatment. The questionnaire consisted of a series of items with questions relating to each of those areas. Employers rated the graduates' performance using a 10-point Likert scale, and these data were collected six months after the students graduated from the program.

The questions asked in surveys generally fall into one of four categories (Jackson, 2008): open-ended, closed-ended, partially open-ended, and Likert rating scales. Table 5.6 illustrates examples of such questions. Each type of question helps us understand in a different way some aspect of learning. Table 5.7 provides additional resources for projects involving surveys.

Experimental

The SoTL designs we discussed in the previous section involved the educational environment. We showed the use of case studies, interviews, focus groups, and surveys to better describe and to provide deeper insight into the way students learn. Such designs are invaluable when studying an environment as complex as the educational environment. However, none of those techniques allows us to conclude whether something we as teachers do actually causes a change. As motivated teachers, we all want to know whether something we did *caused* our students to learn more, change a behavior, improve their attitude, or learn in a deeper way. For us to prove such a causal relationship, we must conduct what is called an experiment.

The experiment we describe is not the kind we may have participated in during a chemistry laboratory, where we combine chemicals and observe reactions; however, this research design shares key similarities with the more commonly thought-of laboratory experiment. Like the chemical experiment, the basic premise of SoTL experiments is that we study a research question or hypothesis, control as much as possible to determine whether a cause-and-effect relationship exists, and do our best not to influence the results. Two groups are always studied in an experiment: a control group and an experimental group. The experimental group is the group that receives a special treatment; the control group does not receive the treatment. In a chemistry

TABLE 5.6
Example of Types of SoTL Survey Questions

Type	Sample Question
Open-ended	Explain how the concept of "objects" transfers to domains outside computing.
Closed-ended	An object is (choose the best answer): a. an instance of a class. b. the same as an attribute. c. the same as a class.
Partially open-ended	Which of the following describes an object (circle all that apply)? a. an instance of a class b. a representation of a person, place, or thing c. an entity with certain characteristics
Likert rating scale	Once I start to work on a program, I find it hard to stop. (strongly agree, agree, neutral, disagree, strongly disagree, not applicable) Rank your comfort in using computers from a scale of 1 (extremely comfortable) to 7 (extremely uncomfortable). 1 2 3 4 5 6 7

laboratory, two solutions would be created to have the exact same composition and, therefore, consistency. They would be stored in the same location at the same temperature and under the same lighting. In our chemistry example, we add ice cubes to one solution but not to the other. The chemist would observe and note the differences in what happens to the two solutions. Because the only difference in treatment was the addition of ice cubes, the chemist could conclude that adding the ice cubes caused any observed change in the solution.

A similar experiment can be designed in educational settings. Recall that Think-Pair-Share is a technique in which students reflect on an answer individually, pair up with another student, and then share their reflections. Suppose we wanted to know whether using the Think-Pair-Share technique actually *caused* students to learn more. To determine a causal

TABLE 5.7
Survey Resources

Books	Sample SoTL Study by Authors	Sample SoTL Study by Others
Fowler, F. J. (2009). *Survey research methods.* Thousand Oaks, CA: Sage; Rea, L. M., & Parker, R. A. (2005). *Designing and conducting survey research: A comprensive guide.* San Francisco, CA: Jossey-Bass; Solomon, D. J. (2001). Conducting web-based surveys. *Practical Assessment, Research & Evaluation, 7*(19). Retrieved May 11, 2010, from http://PAREonline.net/getvn.asp?v=7&n=19	Lynch, J., & Bishop-Clark, C. (1993). Traditional and non-traditional attitudes toward the mixed aged college classroom. *Innovative Higher Education, 18*(3), 109–121.	Denton, B. G., Adams, C. C., Blatt, P. J., & Lorish, C. D. (2000). Does the introduction of problem-based learning change graduate performance outcomes in a professional curriculum? *Journal on Excellence in College Teaching, 11* (2&3), 147–162.

relationship, we could divide the students into two groups. Each group would have the same teacher, the same lecture, the same lighting—essentially all of the identical conditions, but one group would use the Think-Pair-Share technique (experimental group) and the other would not (the control group). One of the most critical elements of this kind of design is control. We attempt to control as much as we can between the two groups so they have the same experience except for the treatment.

One of the hallmarks of experimental design is random assignment of students into groups, which essentially means that each participant has an equal chance of getting into each group. By randomly assigning participants to groups, we help ensure that the two groups are equal when they begin. If they are, and if we keep everything about the education environment the same, then we can conclude that the special teaching technique caused the increased learning.

Experiments are very hard to implement in many educational settings. We often do not have the flexibility to assign students randomly to different groups; however, sometimes we do. In early 2000, the authors studied whether the use of prior e-mail conversations or online discussion groups would lead to better face-to-face discussions (Dietz-Uhler & Bishop-Clark, 2001). We randomly assigned (within one course) students to three groups. The students in group 1 had an Internet chat and then a face-to-face discussion, the students in group 2 had a conversation via a discussion board and then had a face-to-face discussion, and the students in group 3 (control group) simply had the discussion. We randomly assigned students to groups, had two treatment groups and one control group, and were able to draw conclusions about whether we improved conversations. Pate and Miller (2011) similarly randomly assigned students to two groups. One group (the treatment group) used a self-questioning method;

a control group did not. They found that the treatment group scored significantly better on an electrical circuit theory test than did the control group.

While experiments are the only way to infer a causal relationship and are sometimes considered the most "powerful" of research designs, the design itself is not without pitfalls. It is entirely possible that even with random assignment of students, the two groups do not begin as equivalent. It is also possible that over the course of the treatment, something other than the treatment caused the change. For instance, it may not be the Think-Pair-Share activity that caused the change, but instead the teacher was more enthusiastic about all aspects of the learning unit simply because it was the treatment group. While it is beyond the scope of this book to review all reasons why a change may in fact not be due to the treatment, Jackson (2008) provides an excellent and concise review. Table 5.8 provides additional resources for experimental projects.

Quasi-Experimental

While true experimental design is considered the strongest kind of design in that it generates results that are generalizable and imply a causal relationship, true experimental designs are very difficult to implement in many, if not most, educational settings. Recall that the hallmark of an experimental design is random assignment of students to different groups. One group receives some kind of special treatment and the other does not. In medical situations, one cannot randomly assign 100 participants to two groups and assign one group to smoke for 30 years and the other not to smoke. While the ethical implications are not usually as stark in education settings, random assignment is still quite problematic. It is difficult, if not impossible, to assign students randomly to different sections of a course and then test an innovative teaching technique in one class but not the other. Not only is it difficult to

TABLE 5.8 Experimental Resources		
Book	*Sample SoTL Study by Authors*	*Sample SoTL Study by Others*
Campbell, D., & Stanley, J. (1963). *Experimental and quasi-experimental designs for research.* Boston: Houghton Mifflin.	Dietz-Uhler, B., & Lanter, R. (2009). Using the four-questions technique to enhance learning. *Teaching of Psychology, 36,* 38–41.	Pate, M., & Miller, G. (2011). Effects of regulatory self-questioning on secondary-level students' problem-solving performance. *Journal of Agricultural Education, 52*(1), 72–84.

assign students randomly (students sign up for sections of a course based on their schedule), but many of us would have a difficult time withholding a teaching technique that we genuinely believe would help student learning.

While we often cannot assign students randomly to two different groups, we sometimes teach two sections of the same course. At our institution, the authors often teach one day section and one evening section of a popular liberal education course. A natural SoTL project would be to try one kind of teaching technique (for example, Think-Pair-Share) in one section but not in the other and then compare some measure of learning between the two sections. The teacher is the same in both sections of the class, the assignments and exams are the same, and for the most part the course is the same but is delivered at two different times. Think-Pair-Share could be used in the evening section but not in the day section. If the students perform better in the course using Think-Pair-Share, then it seems natural to conclude that the Think-Pair-Share activities led to improved learning. However, the difference between the two groups may not be the Think-Pair-Share activity; it may be that the students signing up for the evening class are simply more motivated. Many SoTL projects are close but not quite experimental in design. These kinds of projects are called quasi-experimental. Quasi-experimental design looks like experimental design but without the random assignment.

Like the other techniques we outlined, many books detail a variety of quasi-experimental designs, including Cook and Campbell's (1979). For our purposes, we briefly outline the quasi-experimental designs often found in SoTL projects: single-group, post-test only; single-group, pre- and post-test; two-group, post-test only; and two-group, pre- and post-test. We apply all four of these designs to answering the question of whether students' learning changed as a result of using the Think-Pair-Share technique.

Single-group, post-test only. This is the simplest kind of quasi-experimental design. One group (a single section of a class) is given a post-test. In fact, this kind of design is the basis for the design of many classes. We teach a topic and then give a quiz or a test to see how well the students mastered the topic. The post-test (or quiz) is meant to evaluate the learning that occurred. Table 5.9 shows the two steps involved in this design. Step one is to try the Think-Pair-Share technique with the entire class and then evaluate that learning with a

TABLE 5.9 Single-Group, Post-Test Only	
Step 1	_Step 2_
Think-Pair-Share	Quiz

TABLE 5.10 Single-Group, Pre- and Post-Test		
Step 1	_Step 2_	_Step 3_
Quiz	Think-Pair-Share	Quiz

quiz. The problem with this kind of design is that we have nothing with which to compare the results. It could be that students performed well on the quiz because they already knew the material. A good performance may have nothing to do with the Think-Pair-Share technique, but everything to do with prior knowledge.

Single-group, pre- and post-test. An improvement over the single-group, post-test only design is the single-group, pre- and post-test, which has one additional step: in this example, the same quiz is given before and after the use of the Think-Pair-Share technique (see Table 5.10). This is an improvement over the previous design, but we still do not know whether using Think-Pair-Share caused an increase in quiz scores. It could be that the lecture that accompanied the Think-Pair-Share made the difference in quiz scores, or perhaps the instructor was more enthusiastic.

Two-group, post-test only. The two-group, post-test only design is similar to the single-group, post-test only design, but a second group is introduced as a comparison (see Table 5.11). For example, we are teaching two sections of the same class and implement the Think-Pair-Share technique in one class but not in the other. We give the same lecture, but in one section we follow that lecture with the Think-Pair-Share and then the quiz, and in the other section we go directly to the quiz. While this begins to look similar to the experimental design, it is important to understand the distinction. Students were not assigned randomly to

TABLE 5.11 Two-Group, Post-Test Only	
Step 1	_Step 2_
Section A: Think-Pair-Share	Quiz
Section B: No Think-Pair Share	Quiz

course sections, so once again it may be that students in one section simply began the course with more prior knowledge.

Two-group, pre- and post-test. The final quasi-experimental design takes the previous example a step further. Table 5.12 shows that this design gives the same quiz both before and after the intervention, and it does so in two different groups. One group uses the Think-Pair-Share, and the other does not. This is almost an experiment; the difference is that there is no random assignment between the two groups. Instead, we compare groups that are together naturally, such as two sections of the same course. Table 5.13 provides additional resources for quasi-experimental projects.

SoTL work is rarely truly experimental in nature. Much SoTL work (in fact, most of ours) has been quasi-experimental and follows one of the designs we previously outlined. However, when the same pre- and post-tests are used across a wide variety of classes with contrasting pedagogies, results can sometimes be obtained that are even more powerful than those from a few experiments (Hake, 1998a; 1998b).

Mixed Methods

Each of the methods described in the preceding section has unique strengths and weaknesses. For example, interviews allow us to understand teaching and learning in depth but often involve only a few people. We cannot assume that what is true for a few students is true for others. On the other hand, an experiment often involves hundreds of students, but the understanding we glean is sometimes superficial. In other words,

TABLE 5.12		
Two-Group, Pre- and Post-Test		
Step 1	*Step 2*	*Step 3*
Quiz	Section A: Think-Pair-Share	Quiz
Quiz	Section B: No Think-Pair-Share	Quiz

through an experiment we can learn that a particular teaching technique helped improve exam scores, but we gain little insight into why the technique improved exam scores. We as educators are well aware that education in the classroom is a highly complex social environment that involves a multitude of factors.

If we use more than one method to study an educational phenomenon, we can have more confidence in our findings and they will be more meaningful. In the majority of our SoTL studies, we used multiple methods. Most often, we used both a qualitative and a quantitative technique in the same study. In the example we use throughout this book, we used focus groups, surveys, and a quasi-experimental approach to better understand the impact of using a novel teaching idea. We used surveys to understand whether the students learned more and what their attitudes were toward the new approach. And we used focus groups to better understand how the new programming language motivated them.

Combining methods is often called *triangulation*, which results in improving educators' understanding of findings. Berg (2007) explains that, as researchers, we each have a preference for a particular research

TABLE 5.13		
Quasi-Experimental Research Resources		
Book	*Sample SoTL Study by Authors*	*Sample SoTL Studies by Others*
Cook, T., & Campbell, D. (1979). *Quasi-experimentation: Design and analysis issues for field settings.* Boston: Wadsworth.	Bishop-Clark, C., Courte, J., & Howard, E. (2006). Programming in pairs with Alice to improve confidence, enjoyment and achievement. *Journal of Educational Computing Research, 34*(2), 213–228.	Iaria, G., & Hubball, H. (2008). Assessing student engagement in small and large classes. *Transformative Dialogues Teaching & Learning Journal, 2*(1), 1–8; O'Loughlin, V. D. (2002). Assessing the effects of using interactive learning activities in a large science class. *Journal of Excellence in College Teaching, 13*(1), 29–42; Weckman, J., & Scudder-Davis, R. (2005). Teaching natural science to nonmajors: A comparison of two different course formats—the "team of experts" vs. the "individual instructor." *Journal of Excellence in College Teaching, 16*(1), 149–169.

method. He explains that each method provides a different line of sight directed toward the same reality, and each line of sight reveals slightly different facets of the same situation. By combining the different lines of sight, we obtain a better, richer, and more complete picture.

Table 5.14 outlines a number of different research questions (all related to the Think-Pair-Share technique) and maps the design methods that may be the most appropriate to answer the question at hand. Keep in mind that you can gain further insight for each question by using multiple methods. Table 5.15 provides additional resources for mixed methods research.

Involving Students

Students can play a valuable role in many aspects of the research design phase. As you sketch out your design,

consider including a team of students whose members help shape that design. As we mentioned in an earlier chapter, the students can be coresearchers throughout the entire process, or they can be involved in a single phase. For instance, if your project focuses on identifying whether students learn more when you use the Think-Pair-Share technique, consider holding a focus group with students about how you should measure whether they learned more. Talk with students to help identify the best kinds of techniques to answer the questions at hand. We come from an entirely different perspective from the students'. And while it sometimes seems obvious to us which methods to use, conversations with students may sway and even completely change our thoughts on how to proceed.

We can involve students in different ways depending on the kinds of techniques we use. Students can be

TABLE 5.14
Research Questions Matched to Design Technique

Research Question	Method
Do students' attitudes toward the unit improve as a result of using the Think-Pair-Share technique?	Quasi-experiment, Survey
Do students who used the Think-Pair-Share technique score higher on a test of content knowledge than those who did not?	Experiment
How does the Think-Pair-Share technique improve learning?	Interviews, Focus Groups, Case Study
Do students enjoy the Think-Pair-Share activity and, if so, why?	Survey, Interviews, Focus Groups
Do students participate more after using the Think-Pair-Share activity?	Observation
How do educators effectively integrate the Think-Pair-Share technique into technical courses such as mathematics?	Descriptive

TABLE 5.15
Mixed Methods Research Resources

Books	Sample SoTL Study by Authors	Sample SoTL Study by Others
Creswell, J. W., & Plano Clark, V. L. (2007). *Designing and conducting mixed methods research.* Thousand Oaks, CA: Sage; Teddlie, C., & Tashakkori, A. (2009). *Foundations of mixed methods research: Integrating quantitative and qualitative approaches in the social and behavioral sciences.* Los Angeles, CA: Sage.	Bishop-Clark, C., Courte, J., Evans, D., & Howard, E. (2007). A quantitative and qualitative investigation of using Alice programming to improve confidence, enjoyment and achievement among non-majors. *Journal of Educational Computing Research, 37*(2), 193–207.	Spezzini, S. (2010). Effects of visual analogies on learner outcomes: Bridging from the known to the unknown. *International Journal for the Scholarship of Teaching and Learning, 4*(2).

trained as interviewers, and the students we are studying may feel more comfortable sharing information with a fellow student than a professor. If we are using a survey, many students are often far more adept at designing web-based surveys and using other recent technologies than we are. Students can review our measures and help ensure they are reliable and valid.

We can train students to observe the classroom and record events in that classroom. Students can be hired to enter data, analyze data, or run complex statistics. In fact, whether your research is descriptive, case study, observation, interview, focus group, survey, experiment, or quasi-experiment, students can play some important and interesting role.

Designing Your Study Worksheet

After you have clearly identified a research question, you move into designing the details of the study. The issues involved in research design are vast and complex. Entire books have been written on a single qualitative method. This worksheet is intended to help you work through several of the primary issues you should consider as you develop your SoTL design.

State your research question.

Identify the type of methodology you will use: qualitative, quantitative, or both.

Will you do a pilot study?

Identify your time frame.

Identify the groups you will study.

Estimate the number of people you will study.

```

```

Consider using comparison groups.

```

```

Identify the approaches you will use.

Qualitative Methods	Quantitative Methods
Descriptive	Survey
Case Study	Experiment
Observation	Quasi-Experiment
Interview	
Focus Group	

Draw your research design. The next two items are intended to be used to clarify in your own mind the exact procedures you will follow as you execute your SoTL research. Many research designs can be illustrated with a picture. If your project can be illustrated with a picture or diagram, draw a picture of your research design.

```

```

Briefly describe your research approach.

```

```

Designing Your Study: Completed Worksheet

After you have clearly identified a research question, you move into designing the details of the study. The issues involved in research design are vast and complex. Entire books have been written on a single qualitative method. This worksheet is intended to help you work through several of the primary issues you should consider as you develop your SoTL design.

State your research question.

> Do students who use the Alice programming language improve their understanding of object-oriented concepts?
>
> Do students who use the Alice programming environment improve their attitudes toward computing?

Identify the type of methodology you will use: qualitative, quantitative, or both.

> Primarily quantitative with some qualitative. Quantitative research is used to determine whether students improved their understanding of object-oriented concepts and whether their attitudes improved. Qualitative research (in the form of focus groups) is used to further understand what the students liked and disliked about the Alice environment.

Will you do a pilot study?

> We will do a pilot study of a small sample for one week. The full study will be 2.5 weeks and will involve several different course sections.

Identify your time frame.

> The time frame is five 75 minute class sessions. The pre-test will take place at the first session, the Alice experience will take place at sessions two through four, and the post-test will take place at the fifth and final session.

Identify the groups you will study.

> The groups studied will be multiple sections of a Computers and Society course. Four different instructors are involved in the study. Each instructor teaches at least one section, and some teach multiple sections. This is a liberal education course, which means a range of students will be represented.

Estimate the number of people you will study.

> Approximately seven to eight sections of 20 students each will be studied. We will hold four different focus groups during the class time for three of those sections.

Consider using comparison groups.

> No comparison groups will be used. Because this is a real classroom activity lasting 2.5 weeks, it would be too disruptive and inconsistent with the goals of the class for some students to experience Alice and for others to experience a different programming environment.

Identify the approaches you will use.

Qualitative Methods	Quantitative Methods
Descriptive	Survey
Case Study	Experiment
Observation	Quasi-Experiment
Interview	
Focus Group	

Draw your research design. The next two items are intended to be used to clarify in your own mind the exact procedures you will follow as you execute your SoTL research. Many research designs can be illustrated with a picture. If your project can be illustrated with a picture or diagram, draw a picture of your research design.

observation (O) ——➤ treatment (T) ——➤ observation (O)

Briefly describe your research approach.

Approximately 120 students in seven different sections of the same course in computer technology will experience a 2.5-week unit that involves the use of the Alice programming environment. Students will be tested on their understanding of object-oriented programming concepts before and after the unit. Similarly, they will be tested on their attitudes toward computer programming before and after the unit. Finally, to glean greater insight into the likes and dislikes of the Alice environment, focus groups will be held in several sections of the course.

6

Collecting the Data

NOW THAT WE HAVE reviewed the types of research design, it is time to start thinking in more detail about how you will collect your data. We make observations and "collect data" all the time. For example, we feel confident when a new activity achieved the intended outcomes because we observe students being fully engaged in the activity. We worry about a recent lecture because we observe the types of questions students ask about it afterward. But these everyday observations, although interesting, are informal, unsystematic, and unconvincing. Now we need to turn these everyday observations into ones that are carefully planned and coordinated (Bordens & Abbott, 2008). The data collection step provides us with an opportunity to think deeply about what evidence we need to show that our students are learning.

You should take a number of detailed considerations into account as you start to design or gather your data collection instruments. First, there are some general issues to consider, such as whether the measurements are good indicators of the variables you want to measure. Second, there are issues to consider about how your variables will be measured. Third, there are nitty-gritty details to consider, such as when the data will be collected, who will collect them, and how they will be collected. Because research is an iterative process, you might decide to change your research question or your research design once you have started thinking about data collection. For example, you might realize that you do not have the resources to collect the kind or amount of data necessary to address your research question, so you might need to go back and revise your research question.

Data collection is a much more complicated component of the SoTL process than I originally realized, which is why assistance and explicit instruction in conducting this kind of research was so helpful. I had previously put together a SoTL project on my own without anyone's help or guidance, and, looking back, I can see that if I had had help, I would have collected the data differently to (1) get answers to the questions I was really asking, and (2) be able to present it more confidently.
—KELLI, ENGLISH

In this chapter, we review the issues to consider when designing your data collection plan, what type of data collection instrument you will need, how to construct your data collection plan, the data collection process, and the ethical issues to consider when using human subjects.

Issues to Consider

As you are thinking about how you will collect your data, there are three general issues to consider. One is the issue of reliability and validity. Reliability refers to the consistency of your measurement instrument, or the degree to which an instrument measures the same thing each time it is used. Basically, reliability refers to the repeatability of your measurement. Why do we want our data collection instrument to be reliable? Suppose a critical-thinking exercise was effective in improving student learning in one class, but not another; or suppose it was effective in the fall semester but not in the spring semester. Not only would situations such as this cause you to worry about how "effectiveness" was measured, but you also might worry about the effectiveness of the critical-thinking activity itself! Validity refers to the strength of our conclusions or propositions. In short, were we right in the conclusions we made about our project? There happen to be many types of reliability and validity (e.g., Bordens & Abbott, 2008; Jackson, 2008; Salkind, 2009), but for our purposes, let's rely on the definitions listed previously.

A second general consideration is how you will define and operationalize your variables. Suppose you are interested in finding out whether test anxiety causes students to perform worse on a final exam. How do you measure "test anxiety"? Suppose you are interested in determining whether the use of clickers in the classroom increases students' confidence in their knowledge of the material. How would you measure "confidence in knowledge of the material"? When defining and operationalizing your variables, it is a good idea to go back to your research question and use it to state explicitly how you will measure your variables. Your research question is usually stated in a specific form such as, "Will students' ability to think critically improve after engaging in a critical-thinking module?" or "Is comprehension of material better for students who completed a reflective activity versus those who did not?" So how do you go about measuring such constructs as "critical-thinking ability" and "comprehension of material"? Be as specific as you can when formulating your measurement plan. For example, critical-thinking ability can be measured by asking students to respond to a critical-thinking question and then applying a critical-thinking rubric to assess it. Comprehension of material can be measured by giving students a quiz that includes both factual and conceptual questions. In a qualitative project on the formation and adherence of a self-disclosure norm (Dietz-Uhler, Bishop-Clark, & Howard, 2005), we defined a norm as more than two self-disclosures or revelations of personal information. We defined and measured adherence to a self-disclosure norm as having a greater number of reinforcing statements in response to a self-disclosure than a non–self-disclosure. Table 6.1 lists some examples of operational definitions of variables.

TABLE 6.1
Examples of Operational Definitions of Variables

Variable	Operational Definition
Enjoyment of an activity	Review ratings of perceived enjoyment (1 = not enjoyable to 5 = very enjoyable). Observe and record the number of smiles while completing an activity. Interview students and ask them questions about their enjoyment of the activity.
Critical thinking	Collect student scores on a critical-thinking rubric applied to an essay. Record the number of evidence-based statements made in class.
Knowledge/learning	Increase in quiz scores from pre-test to post-test. Higher scores on a rubric assessing depth of knowledge in an essay assignment. Improved performance on an oral presentation as measured by a presentation rubric.

A third general consideration is whether to design your own data collection instrument or use a preexisting one. In your search of the literature on studies related to your research question, you probably have found studies that include the same variables that you want to measure in your project. If this is the case, then you will need to decide whether to use the same data collection instrument as the one used in a previous study, adapt it to fit your needs, or design a new one. If you are measuring general constructs such as test anxiety, self-esteem, personality characteristics, etc., it is probably a good idea to use preexisting, published measures because they have already been tried and tested so they are likely to be reliable and valid. For example, in a project on the effectiveness of a critical-thinking exercise in improving students' critical thinking, a preexisting rubric (WSU's Critical and Integrative Thinking Rubric) was applied to students' critical-thinking responses (Dietz-Uhler, 2008). In a project studying whether online discussions led to face-to-face discussions that were perceived to be more enjoyable (Dietz-Uhler & Bishop-Clark, 2001), a measure of "enjoyableness" was developed by asking students how much they enjoyed the discussion, how lively the discussion was, and how satisfied they were with the discussion. Mason, Cohen, Yerushalmi, and Singh (2008) developed a rubric to evaluate physics students' solutions to a problem. The rubric was based on specific criteria, such as physics principles (invoking physical principles and applying physical principles), algebra, and presentation (description, plan/solution construction, and evaluation).

Since I was doing content analysis based on hand-written responses to my questions, I had no choice but to design my own instrument, which I had to construct in order to cover the range of subjects' responses. I could not have known in advance what kinds of things subjects might say. —MARY JANE, ENGLISH

Table 6.2 lists various types of measures, their definitions, and some examples (Jackson, 2008).

Data Collection Plan

Before you can design a detailed plan for data collection, you need to consider the design of your research. In the previous chapter, we discussed in detail nine different types of research designs. Based on those designs, you can try to match your data collection strategy to the design you will use in your project. The following discusses data collection considerations for each of the research designs. (A summary of each data collection method is presented following this section in Table 6.4 on page 74.)

TABLE 6.2 Types of Measurements and Their Definitions			
Type of Test or Measurement	*Definition*	*Example*	*Example Study*
Self-report	A survey or questionnaire that measures an individual's reports of how he or she thinks, feels, or behaves	Items measuring agreement with statements related to enjoyment of a classroom activity	Bishop-Clark et al., 2007
Tests	A test that measures individual differences in ability or personality	Myers-Briggs	Bishop-Clark & Wheeler, 1994
Behavioral measures	Involve systematic observation of behaviors and can include textual, audio, or video recordings	Observing and recording the number of times a person reinforces another person's self-disclosure	Dietz-Uhler, Bishop-Clark, & Howard, 2005
Physical measures	Measure bodily activity, such as heart rate and blood pressure	Measuring a student's heart rate during an exam	Edmonds, 1982

My study involved specific content and bringing the human patient simulator into the classroom for a specific day, which dictated the day I was going to complete the study. —DEBBIE, NURSING

Descriptive

Descriptive research designs can include case studies, observation, interviews, focus groups, and surveys, so be sure to consult the sections that follow for more details. If your research design is descriptive, then data collection involves a description of the issue or topic you want to learn more about. For example, in a study (Bishop-Clark, 2006) about a service-learning project in a class, the data that were collected included written observations and a description of the service-learning project, students' reactions to the project, the reactions of the elementary teacher involved, and the instructor's observations of the class. In a descriptive study about abandoning the lecture in a biology course, Evans and Omaha Boy (1996) collected data on the number of students electing to take a test at the beginning of the course and again at the end. In this case, the data collection was fairly simple.

To prepare for data collection in a descriptive design, you need to decide what information you need to collect in order to describe whatever it is you intend to describe. For example, if you intend to describe an activity you used in class, the data you collect might involve a written description of the goals of the activity, the activity itself, and your observations about it. If your study involves a description of students' reactions to a film, for example, then the data you collect might involve a questionnaire asking students to indicate their responses to the film. When thinking about your data collection plan, try to foresee all the types of information you will need to provide a comprehensive description that will address your research question.

Case Study

A case study involves a description of one person or event or situation. In the case study described in the last chapter, Magolda's (2001) data included students' responses to interview questions that she asked them repeatedly over time. Your case study might include an individual student, event, or class. The type of method you use to collect the data can include interviewing, participant observation, and archival research, for ex-

ample (Willig, 2008). The types of data that are typically collected include excerpts, quotations, passages from records, correspondence, official reports, and open-ended surveys (Patton, 1987). The primary considerations you need to address include deciding which case to select, how you will collect information about that case, and why you chose that particular case (Willig, 2008). Of course, your research question should guide the answers to these questions.

Once you have decided on a case and the types of information you will need to address your research question, you'll need to consider a number of practical data collection issues. First, how will you record the data? If they include textual information, such as from written records or correspondence, consider having them transcribed or scanned so they can be converted to an electronic format. If they involve audio or video recordings, consider how you will transcribe these. Second, figure out whether you can access the information you need. For example, if you want to access student records, will you need to seek permission? Third, determine whether you have the time and money to access the information you need. Some case-based studies involve countless hours at a specialized library and the researcher can amass considerable costs collecting the data.

Observation

If your research question dictates that you engage in some type of observation, then you will need to consider what type of data will best address your question. For example, in a study about the formation of and adherence to a self-disclosure norm in an online chat, our data consisted of an electronic transcript of an online chat (Dietz-Uhler et al., 2005). In this example, our data collection plan was simply to record (using a course-management system) the students' online discussion about the topic. Because we were not sure what type of responses we would get before students engaged in the discussion, it was difficult to design a plan for coding the transcripts.

Depending on the type of observation (e.g., participant observation, observation of live behavior, or observation of recorded information such as online chats or essays), the data can take a variety of forms. If engaging in a participant observation, the data will likely take the form of field notes that are recorded in a field notebook (Mack, Woodsong, MacQueen, Guest, & Namey, 2005). Although field notes are usually textual, they can include maps, diagrams, or organizational charts (Mack et al., 2005). Field notes typically include records of what the observer observes and experiences. It is important to expand field notes as soon as possible after the observation so you do not forget anything. Observational data can also include audio or video recordings.

Participant observation involves several practical issues. First, participant observation usually requires a structured protocol that includes a checklist or rating scale of the types of behaviors and activities of interest (Frechtling & Westat, 1997). It is important to know what you are going to observe in the event or activity or situation. Second, consider who will be acting as the observer(s). If there are multiple participant observers, then they need to be trained to observe the same types of behaviors or actions. Third, it is important to select the site, time, and day (if appropriate), and anticipate how long it will take to make the observations (Mack et al., 2005).

If your research involves observation of live behavior or printed or recorded material, then your data will be different from the data for participant observation. If you are recording live behavior, such as how students cheat during an examination, then your data probably will take the form of frequencies of various forms of cheating. If you will be examining written material, such as student essays or transcripts of a discussion, then your data will also take the form of frequencies of occurrences.

Interviews

As we discussed in the previous chapter, there are many different types of interviews you can use in your project. The types of data that are collected in interviews can include audio and video recordings of the interview, transcripts of these, and interviewer's notes. The types of notes an interviewer takes can contain observations of the interview content, participant behavior, and context (Mack et al., 2005). The types of questions typically used in interviews are open-ended, but close-ended questions can also be included. Of course, there is an art to writing good interview questions. The survey research design section of this chapter details the elements of a good question. Before writing your interview questions, you may want to consult that section. In the previous chapter, we highlighted the advantages of pilot studies. Before finalizing your interview questions, it is a good idea to pilot-test

them. Consider interviewing a couple of students or your colleagues to make sure they understand the questions and that their responses yield the type of data you are looking for. You might be surprised to find that questions that make perfect sense to you do not to someone else.

There are many practical issues to consider before interviewing. Once you have your questions written and pilot-tested, you need to decide how you will record the interview and determine whether you have access to the necessary recording equipment. Usually, interviews are audio recorded and then later transcribed, but it is always a good idea to take notes during the interview in case the audio recording fails and to provide additional information that would not be recorded in an audio recording (e.g., participant's nonverbal behavior, context) (Mack et al, 2005). You also need to decide whom you will interview and what type of informed consent will be necessary. Other decisions include scheduling the interviews, locating a space to conduct them, and deciding who will conduct them. For example, in a study about learning style preferences of physical education majors, Randall and colleagues (1995) audiotaped interviews of 70 students. The study produced 35 hours of taped interviews. Once the audiotapes were transcribed, the researchers ended up with 400 pages of interview data.

Focus Groups

Data collection plans for focus groups are very similar to interviews. It is important to word your interview questions so they produce the kind of data that address your research question. Again, it is important to design your focus group questions so they produce the type of data that address your research question. For example, in a study (Dietz-Uhler, Bishop-Clark, & Fisher, 2002) we did on the effectiveness of online learning, we were interested in students' perceptions of and reactions to online learning. We invited students to attend a focus group in which we asked the following questions:

- What are the characteristics of a "good" course?
- What did you like best about this course?
- What did you like least about this course?
- Compare and contrast your learning experiences in this web-based course to other traditional, face-to-face courses.

- Did you encounter any difficulties with this course? If so, what were they?
- What changes would you suggest for improving this course?
- Would you take another web-based course? Why or why not?

The focus group responses to each of these questions helped us understand, in detail and in depth, students' reactions to and experiences with online learning, as well as how online learning differed from face-to-face learning. The same considerations for designing interview questions apply to focus group questions.

The types of data collected in focus groups are usually in textual form and are recorded through audio, video, and notes taken during the discussion. Mack and colleagues (2005) offer some helpful tips for taking focus group notes, including:

- Create a form on which to write your notes during the focus group.
- Take notes strategically so you are not attempting to write everything verbatim.
- Record participant identifiers so you can identify participants from an audio file.
- Use shorthand, but expand on these notes soon after the focus group.
- Record both the question posed by the moderator and the response.
- Distinguish between participant responses and your own observations.
- Cover a range of observations, including verbal and nonverbal behavior.

As with any data that take the form of field notes or audio or video recording, these data will need to be transcribed and converted to an electronic format.

When we collected data for our focus groups we made sure that the teacher of the class was not in the room. We wanted frank and honest communication about the students' understanding of certain topics and we thought if the instructor were in the room, the students would be a little less open. We had six to ten people in each focus group and we held three of them. Probably the hardest thing about collecting data with the focus group was that sometimes the topic moved in different directions.

We wanted to be able to explore those directions but we also wanted to stay on topic. It was a tricky balance. —CATHERINE, COMPUTER SCIENCE

Practical considerations for focus group designs include determining how you will record the discussion and whether or not you have access to audio or video equipment. Another consideration is deciding who will play the role of the moderator and the note taker. In general, the researcher does not play either of these roles as doing so can lead to biased results. Determining a time, place, and location are also considerations when using a focus group design.

Surveys

As we indicated previously, when using surveys in your project, you often have the option of using an already-published survey. However, if you cannot find or do not want to use a preexisting measure, then you will need to design your own. This section provides some information and prompts about how to design your own self-report measure or test. It also includes details on how to write good interview and focus-group questions. Before designing your own self-report or test, you need to consider a number of issues, including the type of variables, type of questions, and some measurement and practical considerations.

I have collected both quantitative and qualitative attitudinal surveys. I have also collected pre– and post–skill-based assessment data. I collected what I did based upon receiving the data I needed to evaluate the issue of interest within the constraint of the environment in which I was operating. —ERIC, COMPUTER SCIENCE

Consider the type of variable you want to measure. There are two types of variables: discrete, which consists of variables that are usually categorical, such as gender, year in school, or ethnicity; and continuous, which includes variables that fall along a continuum such as quiz scores and attitudes. Why is it important to consider the type of variable you want to measure? First, the type of variable will determine how to design a measurement of it. For example, you probably will not measure "year in school" in a continuous manner by asking respondents to rate their level of "sophomoreness." Second, the type of variable will affect the type of data analysis, which we discuss in the next chapter.

A second consideration is the type of question. Some questions are closed-ended, such as multiple-choice, Likert-scale (e.g., 1 = *disagree* to 5 = *agree*), and yes-or-no questions. Other questions are open-ended, such as "Why are you taking this course?" and "What is the most important concept you learned from this activity?" Deciding on the type of question you use to measure your variables will affect the type of data you get. In general, data from closed-ended questions are easier to analyze, but data from open-ended questions can yield valuable and insightful information.

You should consider several practical and measurement issues when designing your own measurement (Jackson, 2008). First, you should avoid "double-barrel" questions, which are questions that really ask more than one question. For example, the question, "Please indicate the extent of your agreement with the following statement: I found this activity to be enjoyable, worthwhile, and effective." This question is really asking three questions, one about how enjoyable the activity was, one about how worthwhile it was, and another about its effectiveness. Second, you should avoid "leading questions," such as, "Most students find that new technologies enhance learning. Please indicate the extent to which the use of clickers in the classroom enhanced your learning." Finally, it is always a good idea to include any demographic or potentially identifying questions (e.g., predicted grade in the course, year in school, ethnicity) at the end of a survey so respondents will feel more anonymous and freer to respond to the questions. Table 6.3 lists some sample questions we have used in our research.

In survey research, data typically take the form of numbers and, in the case of open-ended items, verbatim data. If you use open-ended questions, then these responses may have to be subjected to content analysis, which we describe in the next chapter. The practical issues to consider when conducting survey research include decisions about the types of questions to include in the survey and whether you will use a preexisting survey, a modified survey, or your own survey. If you intend to write your own survey, then it is a good idea to pilot-test the questions. Another consideration is how to administer the survey. Will it be a paper-and-pencil or electronic survey? You will also need to consider who will administer the survey. If you intend to survey students in your own classes, consider having a colleague administer the survey for you.

I did ask my college-age son to fill out my study questionnaire, and also to help code some responses from students on a small pilot I had done. His feedback was extremely helpful, mostly in confirming that the questionnaire and coding categories were workable. —MARY JANE, ENGLISH

Experiments

As we indicated in the last chapter, experimental research is not very common in SoTL research, primarily because of the difficulty of random assignment. If you have the opportunity to do experimental research, after you've designed the experiment, the next step is to figure out what types of data you will need in order to address your research question. The data you collect might take several different forms. For example, in a study examining the effectiveness of a four-question activity on student learning (Dietz-Uhler & Lanter, 2009), the primary data collected were responses to a five-item, multiple-choice quiz designed to measure the extent of student learning on an activity they had recently engaged in. In this case, the data collection plan involved writing quiz questions.

In another SoTL project (Dietz-Uhler & Bishop-Clark, 2001) that involved an experiment, we investigated the effectiveness of online discussions on subsequent face-to-face discussions. In this study, we were primarily interested in students' perceptions of the face-to-face discussion, so we designed a survey to administer to students after the face-to-face discussion. Most of the questions on the survey were Likert-scale items. Some example questions are:

- How much did you enjoy your group's discussion?
  Not Very Much 1 2 3 4 5 6 7 Very Much
- How "lively" would you rate your group's discussion?
  Not Very Much 1 2 3 4 5 6 7 Very Much
- How much do you think each person contributed to your group's discussion?
  Not Very Much 1 2 3 4 5 6 7 Very Much

TABLE 6.3 Sample Questions							

How much do you think you learned as a result of your group's discussion?

Not Very Much   1   2   3   4   5   6   7   Very Much

How "lively" would you rate your group's discussion?

Not Very Much   1   2   3   4   5   6   7   Very Much

How would you rate the quality of your group's discussion?

Low Quality   1   2   3   4   5   6   7   High Quality

Generally, I have felt secure about computer programming.

Strongly Disagree   1   2   3   4   5   6   7   Strongly Agree

How often do you engage in Internet chats (check one)?

_____ More than 10 times per week

_____ 5–9 times per week

_____ 1–4 times per week

_____ Never

Please rate the frequency of your participation in class discussions in general (check one):

_____ I usually contribute more than my classmates.

_____ I usually contribute about the same as other people in the class.

_____ I rarely contribute to class discussions.

_____ I never contribute to class discussions.

When people are bribed to do what they already like doing, they start to see their actions as externally controlled rather than intrinsically appealing. This is called the

A. foot-in-the-door effect.
B. self-justification effect.
C. overjustification effect.
D. insufficient justification effect.

Explain what happens to people's cognitive development in middle age.

Please answer each of the following demographic questions.

Age: _____

Gender (circle one):   Male   Female

Race (circle one):   White/Caucasian   African American/Black   Asian/Asian American   Hispanic/Latino

          Native American/American Indian   Other _____

Your experiment may involve collecting data that are not in the form of surveys or questionnaires. For example, your study might involve measuring heart rates before a planned exam or a surprise exam. In this case, the data you collect will require the use of a heart rate monitor or some technique to measure heart rate. Your experiment might also involve the use of observation, in which case it is important to design an observation checklist, such as the one we used when observing students in an online chat (Dietz-Uhler et al., 2005).

There are numerous practical issues to consider if you are using an experimental design. These include:

- What type of data collection instrument (e.g., computer, paper and pencil, recording device) will be used.
- Access to and costs of any equipment that might be needed.
- Availability of and access to any physical space necessary to conduct the experiment.
- Recruitment of participants for the experiment (Do you have access to participants? How will you recruit them?).

Quasi-Experiment

The data collection plan for quasi-experimental designs is much the same as for experiments. If your design involves the use of non-preexisting measures, then you will need to design your own data collection instrument. For example, in a project that involved a quasi-experimental design (Dietz-Uhler, 2008), students were asked to complete a questionnaire designed to measure their perceptions of their knowledge of and confidence in critical thinking. Students were then asked to engage in a critical-thinking module designed to improve their knowledge of and confidence in critical thinking. Students were given the same questionnaire that included these and other questions (using a 5-point scale where 1 = *not very* and 5 = *very*):

- How confident are you in using critical thinking?
- How much do you know about critical thinking?

The data collection planning phase of this study involved designing these questions so they adequately addressed our research question.

Wyandotte (2009) was interested in language awareness and critical thinking in students in her English courses. Using a quasi-experimental design in which she tested students' language awareness and critical thinking using a pre- and post-test design over two years, she generated data using impromptu writing assignments. These writing assignments were assessed by two independent raters using a rubric for language awareness and critical thinking. In this case, the data were students' writing samples.

In an interesting study about the effects of Power-

Point presentation handouts on student learning outcomes, Noppe, Achterberg, Duquaine, Huebbe, and Williams (2007) collected data on students' exam performance. Students in one section of the class were given handouts for one exam and one final, while students in another section were given a handout for the final only. This is an example of data collection using data that were already collected for the course.

Mixed Methods

As we mentioned in the last chapter, many SoTL studies involve the use of mixed methods. When planning your data collection, you need to consider carefully the use of different data collection methods. Once you have figured out what types of data collection strategies to use (e.g., survey, interview), you can refer to the previous sections when writing your data collection plan.

Data Collection Process

When you have designed your data collection plan, it is time to start thinking about the details. When will you collect the data? If you are doing this project in your classroom, then your course schedule might dictate when you will be able to collect the data. For example, the study on norm formation and adherence (Dietz-Uhler, Bishop-Clark, & Howard, 2005) required a particular topic (mental health) that was not covered until late in the semester, so the course syllabus dictated the time frame.

> *I collected quiz grades. I gave the same quiz twice, but at different times in my two classes. In one of my classes, I collected the first quiz right after I lectured [and] before the students did the assignment. In the other class, I lectured, the students did the assignment, then I gave the quiz for the first time. I gave both classes the same quiz at the end of the unit.* —JENNIFER, ART HISTORY

Who will administer the questionnaire or survey? This is a practical and ethical issue. On the ethical side, the person teaching the class generally should not administer a questionnaire or survey because all research must be voluntary and students might worry

TABLE 6.4
Summary of Types of Data and Practical Considerations

Research Type	Types of Data	Practical Considerations
Descriptive	Data are in the form of text, audio, video, or numbers (see case study, observation, interview, focus group, and survey for more information about types of descriptive data).	What to describe (case study, observation, and interview are all forms of descriptive data)
Case Study	Data are in the form of text, audio, or video. Data include open- and closed-ended responses, questionnaires, records, excerpts, quotations, correspondence, official reports, and surveys.	Which case to choose What types of information are needed Access to information Time and costs to access and acquire information
Observation	Data are in the form of text, audio, or video. Data include detailed description of activities, participant behaviors, and human interactions.	How to record observations Types of information to record How to transcribe the data The role of the observer
Interview	Data are in the form of text, audio, or video. Data include direct quotes about experiences, feelings, knowledge, and opinions.	How to record interview data Techniques for transcription Questions or topics Type of interview
Focus Group	Data are in the form of text, audio, or video. Data can include detailed description of discussion and notes about context.	How to record focus group data Who will play the roles of moderator and note taker How to transcribe the data
Survey	Data are in the form of numerical responses and verbatim data.	What kinds of questions (write own or use preexisting survey) How to administer the survey When to administer the survey Whom to administer the survey to
Experiment	Numerical responses, verbatim responses, numerical recording.	Data collection instrument (computer, paper and pencil, recording device) Access to and costs of equipment Place/space to conduct experiment Who will participate
Quasi-experiment	Numerical responses, verbatim responses, numerical recording.	Data collection instrument (computer, paper and pencil, recording device) Access to and costs of equipment Place/space to conduct experiment Who will participate
Mixed Methods	Any of the above	Any of the above

that not participating or providing negative feedback will affect their grade if the professor administers the survey. On the practical side, you might have to rely on someone who is available during your class time to administer the questionnaire or survey. Or, if you are trying out a new activity, you might need to rely on a colleague to administer the survey for you. If you are evaluating qualitative data such as papers, essays, or exams, when will you receive that work?

My project involved a multidrafting process in writing, so I had to see where in the syllabus each assignment was due and see how I could incorporate the different drafts into the syllabus. —EVA, SPANISH

We want to point out again that as you start thinking about data collection, you might want to go back and rethink your research design or your research question. Issues may arise in the data collection stage that you did not anticipate when you were thinking about your research question and design. It is acceptable to revise any of the steps of the research process before you begin the project.

Ethical Considerations and IRB

One of the most important considerations in the data collection phase of your research is the ethical treatment of your participants. Any research project involving human or animal participants needs to treat those participants in an ethical manner. In particular, you must consider four primary issues when conducting research with human participants. The first issue is informed consent. Every participant in your study has the right to participate or not participate in your project. In other words, participation has to be voluntary, and there cannot be any negative consequences for deciding not to participate. Participants must also be informed, in as much detail as possible, about what the research involves so they can make an informed decision about whether to participate. One issue that often arises when thinking about informed consent is deception. The American Psychological Association's (1982) Code of Ethics prohibits deception of participants unless it has been determined (by the Institutional Review Board) that deception is warranted given the value of the study and that deception is the only means feasible. In addition, researchers cannot deceive potential participants about aspects of the study that would affect their willingness to participate. Of course, in most research, we might not want our participants to know our hypothesis for fear that it might create demand characteristics, potentially leading participants to respond in ways that confirm the hypothesis. When gaining consent from participants, we can inform them about the purpose of the study without necessarily revealing the hypothesis.

One problem is establishing "tight" or "complete" controls. It might be considered unethical to apply a technique that might improve learning for some students and not for others. One way around this is to compare the current "test" students with those from past semesters or years. This works only if there is a high degree of consistency in instruction and assessment between different years or semesters. —ALAN, ZOOLOGY

The second primary issue is the right to privacy. Every participant in a study has a right to have his or her data remain private. There are two ways to think about privacy. One is the issue of confidentiality. Data are confidential if they are seen only by the researchers. For example, if the data are students' performance on an exam, then the data are confidential if only you (or a research collaborator) can connect exam scores with student names. The other way to think about privacy is anonymity. Data are anonymous if there is no way to attach a name to the data. For example, if your data involved a survey or questionnaire that did not ask for participants' names, and there is no way to identify the respondent based on his or her responses, then these data would be considered anonymous.

The third primary issue is the risk of harm. Every participant in a study has a right to be protected from harm. In research, harm can be physical (e.g., radiation exposure) or psychological (e.g., weakened self-esteem after learning that one performed poorly on a task). Participants in research need to be informed of the potential risks of participating in research. This is not to suggest that research cannot be conducted if there is potential risk. If there is potential risk, then researchers:

1. need to inform participants of the potential risks as well as what options (e.g., interventions, treatments) are available to them should they be harmed, and
2. need to justify that the benefits of conducting the research outweigh the potential risks.

The fourth issue concerns debriefing. Every study participant has a right to learn what the study is about and to learn about his or her role in the research. At this point, you should provide participants with information on how to contact the investigator to learn the results of the study. It is also a good idea to give participants a reference or two to the literature that is related to the study. There is an advantage to the researcher during debriefing as well—he or she might gain insights from participants' comments or perceptions of the research.

In addition to these general ethical requirements of all research, there are some particular ethical issues unique to SoTL research. Hutchings (2003) discusses several issues that SoTL and educational researchers need to consider. One revolves around sharing students' work. If your SoTL project involves students' work, such as papers, presentations, or posters, then you need to obtain students' permission to include this work in your SoTL project. The "sticky" issues revolve around obtaining permission from students. For example, do students really feel free to say no? Are there consequences (immediate and long-term) if they do say no? Can we provide assurance to students that saying no will have no consequence to them?

Another issue that Hutchings (2003) raises is the methodology of the study. For example, perhaps a faculty member believes that using lecture to teach a physics class is not effective because students do not seem to be meeting the outcomes intended for the course. So the faculty member decides to test her hunch by teaching one class using the lecture method (the control group) and another class making use of simulations (the experimental group). The ethical issue is that the faculty member truly believes that the lecture method is ineffective, or at the least, less effective than the simulation method. Is it ethical to teach students using the lecture method if the teacher believes it is less effective than the simulation

method? It seems that doing so is unfair to students in the lecture class.

Often with SoTL studies, we have developed some technique that we believe improves student learning. We have developed this technique to address a difficulty that students have had in the past, and we believe that using these techniques has helped. For the SoTL study we want to demonstrate that this technique, which we believe is effective, really is effective. My understanding is that the strongest way to do this is to split the study group into separate groups, using the new technique with one group and not the other. The ethical, pedagogical issue that I have with this is that I believe that the technique improves student learning and by doing a study in this manner, I have not provided what I believe is the best learning environment for half of my students. Since my primary goal is student learning, I don't perform this type of study. Instead I prefer using a pre-test, treatment, post-test structure where all students receive the same treatment and results are measured within a single group. —ERIC, COMPUTER SCIENCE

It is safe to say that any SoTL project, even just a quick pilot project, requires Institutional Review Board (IRB) approval. The purpose of an IRB is to ensure that researchers are conducting ethical research and that the institution is following government regulations concerning ethical research. But, you might argue, your research should not be subjected to the same scrutiny as laboratory research, for example, because your research involves projects or assignments or exams that you do in class anyway. The IRB recognizes such cases and will allow for exemptions of work involving normal classroom practices. Keep in mind that even if your SoTL project fits in an exempted category, you still need approval from your institution's IRB. If you are not already familiar with this body, it is a good idea to get acquainted with it now.

Coming from a discipline in the humanities, I found all aspects of the IRB to be the most intimidating, including proposing my study according to the guidelines that were more geared for science research and going through the IRB approval

process. The introductory one-hour mandatory session was informative and effective in establishing the importance of having an Institutional Review Board in place to avoid mistreatment of human subjects. The follow-up online training was comprehensive, but I was still unsure about how best to comply with certain requirements. —JENNIFER, ART HISTORY

Some issues you will need to consider to gain IRB approval include:

- Purpose of research (contributions to the existing knowledge base; how the results will be disseminated)
- Description of the subject population (will participants be older than 18 years of age?)
- Research procedures/methods (human subjects protection issues)
- How participants will be recruited and selected
- Consent description (how consent from participants will be obtained; how you will ensure that the voluntary nature of participation is apparent to subjects; how you will implement a system whereby a subject can withdraw from the research aspects of the study without fear of being penalized)
- Nature and timing of the research activities (when participants will participate)
- Procedures for safeguarding confidentiality of information (who will have access to confidential data; for how long will subjects' identifying information be linked to the data; where and how will the data be stored; data security)
- Use of deception (if any)
- Debriefing process
- Potential risks and discomforts (nature and likelihood of risks to subjects; should an identified risk event occur, specifically, what action will be taken to minimize the effect)
- Potential benefits (benefits to participants; benefits to society)

In adhering to a self-disclosure norm study (Dietz-Uhler et al., 2005), careful attention was paid to protecting the confidentiality of the participants. Although the instructor for the course was able to see the actual participants' names, those names were replaced with code names before independent coders viewed the transcripts. In the study on the impact of an online chat on subsequent face-to-face discussions (Dietz-Uhler & Bishop-Clark, 2001), we did not want our participants to know that we were interested in examining how online chats affected later face-to-face ones because we wanted to examine participants' "honest" and unaffected behavior. At the same time, we did not want to deceive participants. In our description of the purpose of the study, we informed participants that the project would examine computer-supported and face-to-face interaction. This description, although honest, was intentionally vague so students could not guess the hypothesis.

You will probably need to take two steps to gain IRB approval. The first, depending on your institution, is to engage in ethics training. For example, you might be asked to complete the CITI Ethics Training Modules (www.citiprogram.org) before you can undertake any research at your institution. Some institutions might also require that you take a practicum before you can initiate any research. Although these training modules and practicums might seem to demand a lot of effort, learning about the ethical treatment of human subjects will help you to protect students and yourself.

The second step is to submit an application to your institution's IRB. You should take a careful look at your institution's IRB form and process as soon as possible. It often takes some time before approval is gained, and you will be unable to start your project until you have approval. You should also recognize that your IRB might not allow you to see your students' data or share the data with students until grades have been submitted. This issue arose for several members of our SoTL Faculty Learning Communities, which elicited some interesting reactions. For example:

I was able to see the data I collected, but I did not know who had given me permission to use the data until after the course was over. Hence, I could not share the data with my students. I thought this was unfair because the students who generated the data had the right to see the results. Nothing was personal; they were commenting on a text and answering quiz questions, something I had done for many incarnations of the course. So I just thought the IRB was being overly cautious. —GINA, SOCIOLOGY

Involving Students in Your Project

In the data collection phase of your project, you can involve students in many ways. First, if you are seeking preexisting measures, your student assistants can help you search the literature to identify potential measures. Of course, your student assistants will need to be savvy in literature searching, but most librarians are eager to assist students engaged in research.

Second, because it is likely that students will be completing your data collection instruments, it would be a good idea to get feedback on your measurements from student assistants. Typically, other students know the language of their classmates better than we do.

Similarly, it is a good idea to test your measures on students or student assistants before you begin data collection. You want to make sure that students can understand the questions and how to answer them. If your project involves the use of papers or exams, it is also a good idea to review these with student assistants to make sure they can understand them.

Third, if ethical issues permit, you can have student assistants help you with data collection. Of course, if your project involves papers, essays, or exams, you probably will not want to have students involved in collecting those. But if your project involves the use of surveys or questionnaires, then student assistants can help you distribute and collect these.

Designing Your Data Collection Plan Worksheet

Now is the time to start thinking about the nitty-gritty details of your SoTL project. The purpose of these prompts is to walk you through the steps that are needed to produce a plan for data collection. You should refer to the information in this chapter to help you address each of the following questions.

To determine how you will define and operationalize your variables, first list the variables in your project.

Second, state in detail how you will operationalize or measure each variable.

What type of research design will you need to use to answer your research question? In the box, state the type of design and the kind of data (e.g., narrative, questionnaire, interview questions) you will need and whether you will design it yourself or use a preexisting measure.

For each of the variables in your project, indicate specifically how you will measure it. Include the questions from your measurement instrument.

In the box, provide detailed information about when, where, and how you will collect your data.

Once you have acquainted yourself with the research compliance requirements at your institution, indicate the steps you need to take to become research compliant (unless you already are), what you still need to learn about the IRB application process, and when you will submit your IRB application.

Designing Your Data Collection Plan: Completed Worksheet

To determine how you will define and operationalize your variables, first list the variables in your project.

> Confidence in programming
>
> Enjoyment of programming
>
> Knowledge of programming

Second, state in detail how you will operationalize or measure each variable.

> Confidence in and enjoyment of programming will be measured by questionnaire items (using a Likert scale where 1 = strongly agree to 5 = strongly disagree) designed to indicate confidence and enjoyment. These two variables will also be measured in a qualitative manner by asking students to participate in a focus group (which will have guided questions) or by completing an essay in response to guided questions. The transcripts of the focus groups and the essays will be coded for evidence of confidence, enjoyment, and knowledge of programming.
>
> Knowledge of programming will be measured by asking students to complete an 11-item multiple-choice quiz about programming.

What type of research design will you need to use to answer your research question? In the box, state the type of design and the kind of data (e.g., narrative, questionnaire, interview questions) you will need and whether you will design it yourself or use a preexisting measure.

> The type of research design is a mixed method design. We will use the survey method and the focus group method to collect the data.
>
> There are several different types of measurements. The quantitative measurements will include questionnaire items to measure confidence in, enjoyment of, and knowledge of programming. Because these measurements are specific to our particular project, we will write our own questions.
>
> For the qualitative measures, we will write our own questions for the focus groups and for the essays.

In the box, state each of the variables in your project and indicate whether it is a discrete or continuous variable.

> Confidence in programming—continuous
>
> Enjoyment of programming—continuous
>
> Knowledge of programming—continuous

For each of the variables in your project, indicate specifically how you will measure it. Include the questions from your measurement instrument.

Coding Guide for the Focus Group Transcripts:
Focus group data were not transcribed and data were not coded. Instead, students were simply questioned in an open-ended way. First, students were asked what they liked about the Alice and the programming unit and what they did not like about them. High-level responses were simply recorded as the students described their likes and dislikes.

Coding Guide for the Essays:
Essays were coded with eight distinct codes. The following is the coding guide used and the phrases looked for to indicate confidence, enjoyment, and achievement or understanding.

Confidence:
1. Easy, simple, comfortable
2. Did more than expected
3. Lack of confidence
4. Fun, entertaining, enjoy, like
5. Imaginative, creative, interesting
6. Dislike the programming process

Achievement/Understanding:
7. Difficulty, complexity, respect for the process
8. Education, learning, understanding

Confidence in Programming (questionnaire items):

(Likert Response: Strongly Agree, Agree, Neutral, Disagree, Strongly Disagree, Not Applicable)

Generally I have felt secure about computer programming.
I am sure that I could learn programming.
I have a lot of self-confidence when it comes to programming.
I am not good at programming.
I am not the type to do well at programming.

Confidence in Programming (essay items):
Essay question: Describe what you liked about Alice and what you did not like.
Analysis: The essays were then coded by two independent raters according to the coding system (codes 1, 2, and 3)

Enjoyment of Programming (questionnaire items):

Questionnaire:
(Likert Response: Strongly Agree, Agree, Neutral, Disagree, Strongly Disagree, Not Applicable)

I like writing computer programs.
Programming is enjoyable.
Once I start trying to work on a program, I find it hard to stop.
The challenge of programming problems does not appeal to me.
Programming is boring.

Knowledge of Programming (multiple-choice items):

Multiple Choice 11-item quiz

Example question: Alice is an example of
  a. machine language.
  b. assembly language.
  c. scripting language.
  d. high-level language.

A property
  a. is an action such as a mouse click or a key press.
  b. always requires a user to respond in a keyboard.
  c. only comes from an external user.
  d. is a property of an object.

Enjoyment of Programming (essay items):
  Essay question: Describe what you liked about Alice and what you did not like.
  Analysis: The essays were then coded by two independent raters according to the coding system (codes 4, 5, and 6).

Knowledge of Programming (essay items):
  Essay question: Do you feel you now understand some of the basics of computer programming?
  Analysis: The essays were then coded by two independent raters according to the coding system (codes 7 and 8).

In the box, provide detailed information about when, where, and how you will collect your data.

The data will be collected in fall and spring semesters in five different sections of the course.

Because the study specifically involves the five-week section of the course on Alice programming, we will collect the pre-test measures prior to this five-week section, and the post-test measures immediately following this five-week section.

The data (questionnaires, multiple-choice quiz, focus groups, or essays) will be collected in each of the nine participating classrooms. The questionnaires and multiple-choice quiz will be distributed to students both before and after the Alice programming unit. The instructor for each of the courses will administer these questionnaires and quizzes. The focus groups will be conducted by two of the researchers, but the instructor will not be present. The essays will be administered by the instructor of the class.

Once you have acquainted yourself with the research compliance requirements at your institution, indicate the steps you need to take to become research compliant (unless you already are), what you still need to learn about the IRB application process, and when you will submit your IRB application.

All of the researchers involved have already completed the training required at our university (this includes CITI training and a one-hour practicum). In addition, we have submitted our IRB proposal and have received approval to conduct the study.

Analyzing the Data

THE NEXT STEP in a SoTL project, analyzing the data, is probably the most exciting step in the SoTL process. We have posed our question, chosen a research design, collected data, and now we get to find out the answer to our research question! We find this step one of the most interesting for this very reason. As we discovered in our faculty learning communities, participants were excited to learn the answer to their research question, to find out whether their hunches about student learning were confirmed, and to determine whether their new teaching method was effective in improving student learning. But they were less excited about "data analysis." Many participants in our learning community who completed SoTL projects that involved quantitative data were nervous about statistics, as they had little experience with these tools. Participants whose SoTL projects involved qualitative data reported uncertainty about how to analyze those data systematically. On the other hand, several participants felt comfortable analyzing both types of data.

This chapter is not intended to provide all of the information you will need to analyze your data, whether they are qualitative or quantitative. Instead, it is meant to help you think through your data analysis and to give you a start on what you need to do to analyze your data. We begin this chapter with a couple of prefaces. First, we assume that you are a novice when it comes to understanding data analysis. If you have advanced knowledge and experience with data analysis, then we hope this chapter will not insult you. Sec-

ond, this chapter is not written with the expectation that you will analyze your own data (although it will provide you with the knowledge to be able to do so, assuming that your data analysis is not especially complex). If you do not wish to become a capable data analyst, then we encourage you to rely on colleagues who are or on a statistical consulting center at your college or university.

In this chapter, we cover such topics as why it is valuable to know about data analysis, basic concepts in qualitative and quantitative data analysis, and involvement of students in this step of the research process. More specifically, the chapter is divided into two main sections, each covering basic concepts of qualitative and quantitative data analysis. Table 7.1 provides a more detailed organization of the topics and issues covered in this chapter, aligned with the research designs that were covered in chapters 5 and 6.

Why Do I Need to Know About Data Analysis?

Imagine walking into your doctor's office to discuss treatment for an illness. Your doctor advises you to use a particular medication to treat the illness. You ask the doctor, "Will this treatment cure my illness?" Your doctor responds that it probably will cure the illness. You ask the doctor, "How do you know it probably will cure my illness?" Your doctor tells you that he has

	TABLE 7.1	
	Summary of Data Analysis Strategies	
Research Type	*Types of Data*	*Data Analysis*
Descriptive	Data are in the form of text, audio, video, or numbers (see case study, observation, interview, focus group, and survey for more information about types of descriptive data).	Narrative analysis Rubric analysis Computing descriptive statistics
Case Study	Data are in the form of text, audio, or video. Data include open- and closed-ended responses, questionnaires, records, excerpts, quotations, correspondence, official reports, and surveys.	Narrative analysis
Observation	Data are in the form of text, audio, or video. Data include detailed description of activities, participant behaviors, and human interactions.	Narrative analysis Computing descriptive statistics
Interview	Data are in the form of text, audio, or video. Data include direct quotes about experiences, feelings, knowledge, and opinions.	Narrative analysis
Focus Group	Data are in the form of text, audio, or video. Data can include detailed description of discussion and notes about context.	Narrative analysis
Survey	Data are in the form of numerical responses and verbatim data.	Computing descriptive statistics Computing inferential statistics Narrative analysis
Experiment	Numerical responses, verbatim responses, numerical recording	Computing descriptive statistics Computing inferential statistics
Quasi-experiment	Numerical responses, verbatim responses, numerical recording	Computing descriptive statistics Computing inferential statistics
Mixed Methods	Any of the above	Any of the above

tried it with a couple of patients and thinks it works pretty well. Clearly, this statement is not very convincing. We would much prefer that our doctor told us about scientific studies that investigated the effectiveness of the treatment. The point is that we would not settle for opinions or anecdotal evidence in many matters, so why would we want to when it comes to teaching and learning? If you want to convince your colleagues, students, and others in your field that your project is effective, you will need an effective research design, and, to be convincing, you will need to provide your colleagues, students, and others in the field with effective data analysis.

Simple statistics are usually used for quantitative data to compare means (parametric if possible, otherwise nonparametric). Graphs also are important to visualize the data and enhance communications with others. These analyses usually are straightforward and with few issues. The qualitative data do raise issues and often are fairly idiosyncratic.

There are basically two good reasons why you need
to know about data analysis. The first is that if you are
a *consumer* of the scholarship of teaching and learning,
knowledge of statistical analysis will allow you to be
more critical and better informed about the study. For
example, consider this paragraph from the results
section in a journal article (Bishop-Clark et al., 2007).
(For those not familiar with statistical terminology,
note that *SD* refers to standard deviation, which is a
measure of the variability; *p* refers to a probability
level, and *t* refers to a test statistic called a "*t*-test." In
general, when a probability level is less than .05, we
can be confident that the result is unlikely to have occurred by chance.)

> In both the spring and the fall, students were
> more confident in programming after their ex-
> perience using Alice, more so during their fall
> experience. In the fall semester, the students had
> a mean confidence score of 3.16 (SD = .69) prior
> to their Alice experience and a mean confidence
> score of 3.44 (SD = .09) after indicating a signif-
> icant improvement in confidence, $t(43)$ = –2.81,
> p = .007. Similarly, in the spring semester, the
> study participants had a mean confidence score
> of 3.3 (SD = .72) prior to their Alice experience
> and a mean confidence score of 3.52 (SD = .67)
> after, indicating a slight improvement in confi-
> dence, $t(78)$ = –1.61, p = .112.

Less statistically inclined audiences are likely to understand the text that precedes each mention of statistical
terms (e.g., "In both the spring and the fall, students
were more confident in programming after their experience using Alice, more so during their fall experience"). If you pay attention only to the text, you are
relying solely on the researchers' interpretation of the
results. But if you understand the statistics the researchers are reporting, you might obtain a more complex picture of the results. For example, note that in
the last result ("Similarly, in the spring semester, the
study participants had a mean confidence score of 3.3

[SD = .72] prior to their Alice experience and a mean
confidence score of 3.52 [SD = .67] after, indicating a
slight improvement in confidence, $t[78]$ = –1.61, p =
.112."), the *p*-level looks different from the other reported results. What does this mean? It means that the
difference between the pre-test mean (3.30) is not *significantly* different from the post-test mean (3.52).
Did the researchers provide any clues to indicate these
means were not significantly different? Yes, when they
stated that the results indicated "slight improvement."
Still, the statistics provide a richer picture of results
than the text alone does.

The second reason you need to know about data
analysis is because you are going to be a *producer* of the
scholarship of teaching and learning. Having basic
knowledge of data analysis will make your reporting
more convincing. Although you might rely on a colleague, student, or statistical consultant to analyze
your data, you will still need to have some understanding of data analysis so you can write the results and
provide an accurate and appropriate interpretation of
those results.

Basic Concepts in Qualitative Data Analysis

Qualitative data analysis is guided by many different
qualitative methodologies and "traditions" (e.g.,
Creswell & Plano Clark, 2007). Many of these methodologies are too complex to cover in this brief chapter;
therefore, we highlight some general principles about
qualitative data analysis. If your research design is qualitative (descriptive, case study, observation, interview, or
focus group), then you will need to rely on qualitative data analysis procedures. For those whose fields
don't usually engage in qualitative analysis, it consists of
analysis of text, verbatim comments, and observation,
not numbers. Although all data analysis involves interpretation, qualitative data analysis involves a high degree of interpretation (Taylor-Powell & Renner, 2003).

One of the exciting aspects of qualitative data is that you get an opportunity to read students' works and their responses to your questions, to delve into data that might reveal how students are thinking and how they are learning. There are many qualitative data analysis techniques for making sense of qualitative data, but the "story" you end up telling is based on your (informed) interpretation of the data. Figuring out and understanding this story is one of the most exciting features of qualitative data analysis!

Steps in Qualitative Data Analysis

Regardless of the type of qualitative data, there are several steps to take (Taylor-Powell & Renner, 2003). Many of these steps will be fleshed out in greater detail in the sections that follow. The basic steps include:

1. *Spend time getting to know your data.* It is important to read and re-read your interview transcripts, field notes, focus group notes, etc., so you really know what types of information you have. During this step, you should consider whether you will need all of the data you've collected and if some data are more valuable than others.
2. *Be mindful of your research question.* We have made this point previously but it bears repeating. It is easy to get bogged down and overwhelmed by the amount of data you have, so it is helpful to remind yourself of the research question so you can focus your analysis.
3. *Look for categories or themes in your data.* As we will discuss, how you identify categories or themes in your data can depend on whether you are doing inductive or deductive content analysis. It is in this step that you are really engaging in the *analysis* part of your data.
4. *Examine the data for patterns and connections between themes and categories.* The goal of any data analysis is to be able to tell a coherent story about your data as they relate to your research question. Your data analysis probably will involve reading and re-reading your data to identify themes and categories. Try to establish connections between your themes or categories so you can explain your data in a coherent and unified fashion. This process is

often referred to as the constant comparative method (Glaser & Strauss, 1967). The primary goal of this method is to systematically compare the data or text assigned to each category so that you attain a full understanding of the meaning of that category. This process also allows for integration of the categories into a unified theme.

5. *Interpret and explain your data.* In this last step of the data analysis process, the goal is to interpret the data. Some questions to ask at this point include: Why are these data important? What is the primary lesson learned with these data? How do these data address your research question?

Preparing Your Data for Analysis

Qualitative data can include field notes from observations, audio and video recordings of interviews and focus groups, and quotations and artifact data from case studies, for example. Regardless of the type of data, preparing your data for analysis involves organizing them into a manageable form (Taylor-Powell & Renner, 2003). Consider adding identifying numbers to interviews, respondents, or observation sessions. If your data are in the format of audio recordings, then these will need to be transcribed into an electronic or written format. One consideration is the amount of data you have. If your narrative data are relatively small in quantity (e.g., if you did a couple of short interviews with students), you might be able to transcribe them yourself. If your data set is large, consider having someone transcribe it for you. Of course, many software programs are available to assist you with this process. Table 7.2 offers some websites to consider for this process. Be sure to keep all identifying information, such as the source of the data, the individual, the site, etc., with the data (Taylor-Powell & Renner, 2003).

For example, in the study on how much students learned from a new programming method, Bishop-Clark and colleagues (2007) used a variety of methods to collect the data. One method involved asking students to answer essay questions to assess their knowledge of the principles used in Alice programming. Questions included: "How are algorithms related to what you did in Alice? What is the relationship between the symbols in a flowchart and the stories you created in your labs? Can algorithms help you create

TABLE 7.2 Data Transcription Software	
Name of Program	*Website*
Digital Research Tools Wiki (repository of data transcription software links)	https://digitalresearchtools.pbworks.com/w/page/ 17801711/Transcription%20Tools
Dragon	www.nuance.com/naturallyspeaking
HyperTRANSCRIBE	www.researchware.com/products/ hypertranscribe.html

better Alice stories? Explain." The researchers asked students to type their responses using Word, which allowed them to have an electronic copy of each student's responses. To give you a sense of the type of data they had, the following is a portion of one student's response:

Algorithms are related to what I did in Alice because they both consist of a set of procedures. The set of procedures in an algorithm consists of instructions just like in Alice. In Alice you need a starting place for your procedure just like you need in an algorithm. Another way algorithms are related to Alice is they both have steps that repeat each other. The relationship between the symbols in a flowchart and the stories I created in my lab would be they both are done in that order . . . .

Because the data were already in electronic format, there were a number of different ways the researchers could have managed them. One is to print out each student's responses and analyze the data in paper format. Another method is to cut and paste the responses into an Excel spreadsheet, for example, and analyze the data in electronic format. We discuss each of the methods for this particular example in the following section.

Your data might be best analyzed in a word processing program (such as Word) or in a spreadsheet (such as Excel). There are software programs to analyze qualitative data, including, for example, programs such as Ethnograph or NUD*IST or NVivo (Davies, 2007). These programs facilitate the steps for qualitative data analysis (Taylor-Powell & Renner, 2003). Table 7.3 includes some web links to these types of software. Randall, Buschner, and Swerkes (1995) used software to assist with the analysis of the interview data they collected from physical education majors. After transcribing the data and using the constant comparison method to sort the data into categories, they refined their analysis further with software that allowed them to sort the data.

TABLE 7.3 Qualitative Data Analysis Software		
Software Name	*Purpose*	*URL*
Ethnograph	Collects data, codes data, writes memos, and analyzes data.	www.qualisresearch.com
NVivo	Sorts and analyzes audio files, videos, digital photos, and text.	www.qsrinternational.com/products_ nvivo.aspx
NUD*IST	Sorts and analyzes audio files, videos, digital photos, and text.	www.qsrinternational.com/products_ previous-products_n6.aspx

I do feel like I'm kind of "out there on my own" in some ways on the qualitative analysis. I purchased qualitative software and am beginning to familiarize myself with that resource. I do feel competent enough to draw general conclusions, recognize themes, and highlight student responses. I just want to be sure that I've mustered plenty of rigor before submitting manuscripts. —BROOKE, NURSING

Narrative Analysis

One way to think about qualitative data analysis is that qualitative data are on a continuum, from being highly qualitative (e.g., reflective analysis) to being almost quantitative (where data are in the form of counts or frequencies) (Tere, 2006). The types of data collected in case studies, observations, interviews, and focus groups are textual and will need to be subjected to some type of narrative analysis. Narrative analysis is typically referred to as content analysis (Taylor-Powell & Renner, 2003). Content analysis is used when we want to analyze a written or spoken record of specific categories (e.g., pauses in speech), items (e.g., negative comments), or behavior (e.g., factual information offered during a group discussion).

There are three basic characteristics of content analysis. The first is objectivity: information is categorized and quantified by clear rules. How you decide on the categories to use is entirely up to you, but in general, the categories are either inductive or deductive (Patton, 1987). Inductive content analysis involves carefully reading the text and identifying the categories or themes that emerge (Mayring, 2000; Patton, 1987). For example, in the project examining the formation and adherence of a self-disclosure norm in an online chat, Dietz-Uhler, Bishop-Clark, and Howard (2005) had to spend time reading through the transcripts to decide on the categories that emerged. The following is an excerpt from that online discussion in which we have disguised names and modified some of the facts to protect identities.

245 **Heather** > My father is recovering, for 23 years now.

246 **Marsha** > I don't mean to say everyone is like that but my brother's illness stemmed from the death of our parents several years ago and he won't seek help even though we have tried

247 **Sue** > my brother lost his arm in a car accident and was never the same.

248 **Beth** > That is so frustrating—when help is there but isn't taken.

249 **Sue** > he died at age 27

250 **Cynthia** > that's real young

251 **Cathie** > Unfortunately, I've noticed men are more reticent to see psychologists because it hurts their macho image

252 **Heather** > This is getting upsetting.

253 **Sue** > my other brother died at age 18

254 **Heather** > Sue, how?

255 **Cynthia** > what from?

256 **Beth** > Sue, you have had a lot to deal with.

257 **Sue** > he was hit by lightning.

258 **Sue** > instant death

259 **Lisa** > My daughter had bulimia in college and for me I felt like a failure. That I was a terrible parent.

260 **Sue** > yes, I have, Beth . . . but I think I am OK

261 **Marsha** > I'm sorry Sue

262 **Sue** > I couldn't imagine that, Lisa

263 **Pamela** > Yes, Lisa . . . I feel the same way about my daughter

264 **Heather** > I have a sister who had anorexia in college.

Once we determined the categories, we had to "code" a number of different variables. Table 7.4 includes the coding scheme we used to code each contribution in the discussion.

TABLE 7. 4
Example Coding Scheme

Name	Name of Student (first name only)
Self-disclosure	0 = no, 1 = yes
Request for self-disclosure	0 = no, 1 = yes
Statement supportive of self-disclosure	0 = no, 1 = yes
Statement supportive of non–self-disclosure	0 = no, 1 = yes
Number of words	

It is important to bear in mind that our "read" of the data was driven exclusively by our research question. We wanted to know how norms in online discussions emerge and are maintained. Regardless of whether your data are interview transcripts, field notes, observations, or archival records, you should read and review them carefully in light of your research question. In inductive content analysis, always ask yourself what types of categories or patterns you need to observe in your data to answer your research question.

Deductive content analysis involves the use of preexisting categories that have typically been formulated by a theory (Mayring, 2000). For example, in a study examining the types of self-reflection in nursing students' journals, Wong, Kember, Chung, and Yan (2005) modified a preexisting self-reflection coding scheme (Boud, Keogh, & Walker, 1985) to content code students' journal entries. The coding scheme they used is portrayed in Table 7.5 (Wong et al., p. 57).

TABLE 7.5
Self-Reflection Coding Scheme

Code	Elements of Reflective Practice	Criteria
1	Attending to feelings	Using positive feelings Removing obstructing feelings
2	Association	Linking of prior knowledge, feelings, or attitudes with new knowledge, feelings, or attitudes Discovering prior knowledge, feelings, or attitudes that are no longer consistent with new knowledge, feelings, or attitudes Reassessing prior knowledge, feelings, or attitudes and modifying them to accommodate new knowledge, feelings, or attitudes
3	Integration	Seeking the nature of relationships of prior knowledge, feelings, or attitudes with new knowledge, feelings, or attitudes Arriving at insights
4	Validation	Testing for internal consistency between new appreciations and prior knowledge or beliefs
5	Appropriation	Making knowledge one's own New knowledge, feelings, or attitude entering into own sense of identity New knowledge, feelings, or attitudes becoming a significant force in own life
6	Outcome of reflection	Transformation in perspectives Change in behavior Readiness for application Commitment to action

Rubric Analysis

In SoTL research, we often use preexisting rubrics to content-code students' written work. Applying a rubric to score students' written responses is a form of deductive content analysis. Rubrics, the criteria you use to evaluate student work, are the explicitly stated guidelines you use to identify various components and levels of student work. Typically, rubrics are used to evaluate qualitative data, such as papers, essays, and presentations.

Here are just a few of the many good resources for you to explore:

- Rubistar: http://rubistar.4teachers.org/index.php
- Landmark Rubric Builder: http://landmark-project.com/rubric_builder
- Rubrics.com: http://rubrics.com

Figure 7.1 includes a portion of the Washington State Critical Thinking Rubric (WSU's Critical and Integrative Thinking Rubric, 2010), which we have used in our research.

The second characteristic of content analysis is that the procedure is systematic. Information is assigned to categories according to whatever rules are developed. Finally, content analysis is general. The findings should fit within a theoretical or applied context.

*Professor Howard and I carefully reviewed the coding procedure to make sure we were using the same logic. I coded all essays. Professor Howard coded 25% of the same information to determine coder reliability. A colleague ran the statistics to make sure that our coding was reliable. We had 10 variables coded as a 0 or 1. Zero indicates the variable was absent and 1 indicates the variable is present. The process went very smoothly after we established common logic. It was very helpful that Professor Howard and I had worked together often and could communicate efficiently. —*DONNA, COMPUTER SCIENCE

In the study by Bishop-Clark and colleagues (2007), some of the data included students' responses to essay questions. As we mentioned previously, a number of methods could have been used to organize the data for analysis. Using the paper method, coders would read each of the responses and score them on the paper copy, according to the scoring scheme (see Table 7.6) they created. Using this method, they would likely need to create a *data summary sheet* (described on page 94 in the "Preparing Your Data for Analysis" section in the quantitative data analysis section of this chapter). Another method would be to cut and paste responses into an Excel spreadsheet and have coders enter their scoring codes there.

Mason et al. (2008) were interested in studying diagnostic skills of physics students. In their study, they gave students a problem to solve that required the students to use particular knowledge learned in class to solve the problem. Their solutions were scored based on a rubric created for the study. The rubric was based on specific criteria, such as physics principles (invoking physical principles and applying physical principles), algebra, and presentation (description, plan/solution construction, and evaluation). This study is particularly interesting because both the researcher and the student used the rubric to evaluate the students' solutions.

Another important issue is establishing reliability in the coding. If the researcher alone or only one person codes or interprets the data, then the resulting codes or interpretation might be biased. At least two people need to review the data and agree on its interpretation.

	TABLE 7.6 Coding Scheme		
Score	0–1	2–3	4
Criteria	Incomplete or incorrect explanation; response does not show reflective thought.	Essay is a good start but not well thought out or well organized. Response needs additional clarification or explanation. Length is not appropriate.	Essay is complete, well written, thorough, and grammatically correct. No spelling errors or typos.

1. Identifies, summarizes (and appropriately reformulates) the **problem, question, or issue.**

Emerging		Developing		Mastering	
1	**2**	**3**	**4**	**5**	**6**
Does not attempt to or fails to identify and summarize accurately.		Summarizes issue, though some aspects are incorrect or confused. Nuances and key details are missing or glossed over.		Clearly identifies the challenge and subsidiary, embedded, or implicit aspects of the issue. Identifies integral relationships essential to analyzing the issue.	
Comments:					

2. Develops, presents, and communicates OWN **perspective, hypothesis, or position.**

Emerging		Developing		Mastering	
1	**2**	**3**	**4**	**5**	**6**
Position or hypothesis is clearly inherited or adopted with little original consideration.		Position includes some original thinking that acknowledges, refutes, synthesizes, or extends other assertions, although some aspects may have been adopted.		Position demonstrates ownership of constructing knowledge or framing original questions, integrating objective analysis, and intuition.	
Addresses a single source or view of the argument, failing to clarify the established position relative to one's own.		Presents own position or hypothesis, though inconsistently.		Appropriately identifies own position on the issue, drawing support from experience and information not available from assigned sources.	
Fails to present and justify own opinion or forward hypothesis.		Presents and justifies own position without addressing other views, or does so superficially.		Clearly presents and justifies own view or hypothesis while qualifying or integrating contrary views or interpretations.	
Position or hypothesis is unclear or simplistic.		Position or hypothesis is generally clear, although gaps may exist.		Position or hypothesis demonstrates sophisticated, integrative thought and is developed clearly throughout.	
Comments:					

Figure 7.1.   Critical Thinking Rubric

In general, if the reviewers or coders agree at least 80% of the time, then the interpretation or coding is deemed reliable.

Developing coding categories was not too difficult, once I read through all the responses to the questionnaire; the challenging part was establishing some reliability in coding with my student coders. We followed the standard process of having the student assistants code part of the responses and compare their code decisions until their ratings matched 80% of the time. One question in particular proved difficult for the coders to rate similarly; if I were to do this study again, I would revise that particular question. I learned from this process overall that content-analysis studies should probably be designed in two parts, one as a pilot just to test the questionnaire and coding categories with actual student coders, and the second for the actual study. —MARY JANE, ENGLISH

Basic Concepts in Quantitative Data Analysis

This section is meant to provide you with some basic definitions and common language of statistics so you can be a more informed consumer and producer of statistics, if you're not already. *Statistics* refers to the set of methods and rules used for organizing, summarizing, and interpreting information (Kiess & Green, 2010). Statistical procedures help to ensure that information and observations (i.e., data) are presented in a systematic and informative manner. Statistics also provide researchers with a common language and a set of standardized techniques that everyone in the research community recognizes and understands.

Preparing Your Data for Analysis

So let's imagine that you have completed the data collection phase of your project. You probably have sitting on your desk a stack of questionnaires that students completed, a pile of essays to which you need to apply a rubric to produce numbers, or exams that need to be graded. What do you do with all this paper? First, all of these "data" need to be converted into a numerical and analyzable format. If your data are quantitative (e.g., closed-ended survey questions or exam scores), then your task is simple because your data are already in numerical format.

Once you have your data in numerical format, you can transfer those numbers to a *data summary sheet*, which allows you to compile your data. There are two ways to produce a data summary sheet. One is to create a summary sheet using word-processing software and then enter the data by hand. Table 7.7 is an example of a data summary sheet for a study on attitudes toward online learning. You could print out something like this and then enter the numbers by hand.

Of course, it is highly likely that your data will need to be entered into a statistical software program. If you are savvy enough with Excel, for example, you could transfer the data directly from the questionnaire or essays or coded transcripts into an Excel spreadsheet. Figure 7.2 portrays an example of an Excel spreadsheet with the codes for the norm formation study (Dietz-Uhler et al., 2005).

TABLE 7.7
Example Data Summary Sheet

Respondent Number	Q1: Enjoyable rating	Q2: Difficulty rating	Q3: Use of technology rating	Q4: Perceived learning rating
1				
2				
3				
4				
5				
6				
7				

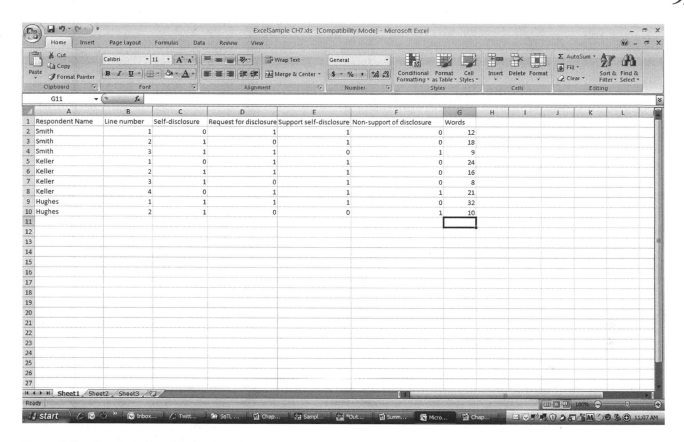

Figure 7.2. Example Excel Data File

Descriptive Statistics

Statistics basically serve two purposes: to describe data and to make inferences about data. (We explain descriptive statistics here and inferential statistics in the next section.) *Descriptive statistics* describe raw data in the form of graphics or sample statistics (Bennett, Briggs, & Triola, 2009). There are several different types of descriptive statistics, which generally can be categorized as frequency distributions and graphs, measures of central tendency, and measures of variability. You probably are already familiar with all three of these categories, but you may not be as comfortable with the statistical jargon.

Frequency distributions are basically counts of the number of scores. For example, when looking at scores on an exam, we often look at how the scores are distributed. One way to do that is to look at a frequency distribution. Table 7.8 is a fictitious example of a basic frequency distribution of exam scores for a study looking at the effects of an activity on learning. Note that there are many different types of frequency distributions, but for our purposes, we will look at the simplest form.

| | TABLE 7.8 | |
| | **Frequency Distribution Table** | |
Score	*Frequency*	*Percentage*
85	3	5
84	3	5
83	5	9
82	4	7
81	5	9

When you collect your data, you probably will want to construct a frequency distribution so you can "see" what your data look like. Of course, some people are more visual than others and prefer to "see" their data in the form of *graphs*. Just like with frequency distributions, there are many different types of graphs. Figure 7.3 is an example of a histogram, which provides the same information as the frequency distribution, but does so in a picture rather than a table.

Another category of descriptive statistics is *measures of central tendency*, which are numbers that represent the typical score obtained on each of the measures (Kiess & Green, 2010). There are three different measures of central tendency. The first is the mean, which is the sum of all of the scores divided by the total number of scores. The median is the score that lies in the middle of the distribution, although it is technically defined as the score in a distribution with an equal number of scores above and below it. Finally, the mode is the most frequently occurring score in a distribution. How do you know which measure of central tendency to use? Well, it depends on the type of measurement you are using and the shape of your frequency distribution, both considerations of which are beyond the scope of this chapter. Table 7.9 includes all

TABLE 7.9	
Descriptive Statistics: Measures of Central Tendency	
Mean	78.53
Median	78.00
Mode	77.00

three measures of central tendency for our fictitious exam data.

The third category of descriptive statistics is *measures of variability*. Variability refers to how much the scores in a distribution vary from one another as well as from the measure of central tendency. In short, they tell us how different the scores are from one another. The most frequently computed and reported measures of variability are the range, variance, and standard deviation. The range is the difference between the highest and lowest score. The variance is computed by subtracting each of the scores in a distribution from the mean score, squaring those scores, and then adding them all up. (The reason for squaring the scores is so that you do not end up with negative scores.) Finally, the standard deviation is the square root of the variance. This measure of variability is especially valuable because it is in the same unit of measure-

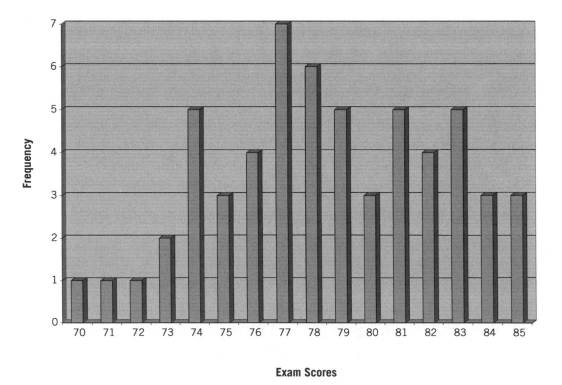

Figure 7.3. Example Histogram

ment as the scores, so it allows us to say such things as, "The mean on the exam was 78.53 and students scored within plus or minus 3.79 points of the mean." Table 7.10 includes all three measures of variability from our fictitious study of exam scores.

TABLE 7.10	
Descriptive Statistics: Measures of Variability	
Range	15.00
Variance	14.36
Standard Deviation	3.79

Inferential Statistics

Inferential statistics refers to procedures for making inferences about a population. For example, based on the data from your sample, which is a subset of a larger population, you want to know how likely you are to be able to generalize to the larger population. Before describing the types of inferential statistics, it is helpful to know something about *statistical significance*. When we collect data from our sample, we assume that our population has particular characteristics with regard to measures of central tendency (averages) and variability (spread of scores). Given that our population has certain characteristics, what is the chance (this is the *p*-value we referred to earlier) that we would see data that contradict the assumptions? In statistical terms, we test the null hypothesis that our sample does come from the assumed population against the alternative hypothesis that our sample is from a different population. As odd as it may seem, we want to reject the null hypothesis in favor of the alternative hypothesis. For example, if I want to test a new activity to improve critical-thinking scores, my null hypothesis is that my sample is from a population of students who do *not* have improved critical thinking, and my alternative hypothesis is that my sample is from a population of students who do have improved critical-thinking scores. Why do I want to reject the null hypothesis that there is no difference between my sample and the assumed population? Because it is easier to show that something is false than it is to show that it is true. For example, if I want to test the hypothesis that all dogs have four legs, I only need to find one three-legged dog to show that this hypothesis is false. Getting back to our question of what the chance is that we would see data that contradicted the assumptions we make about a population, if that chance is small (e.g., the probability [*p*] is .04), then we conclude that our assumptions about the population were flawed and our sample probably has not come from our assumed population. If the chance is not small (e.g., *p* = .63), then we conclude that our assumptions about the population were not flawed or that there is no overwhelming reason for us to reject our initial assumptions. In more

everyday language, statistical significance refers to whether our sample differs from our population. As we mentioned earlier, we usually want it to be different. For example, we want scores on an exam to be different after students have engaged in an activity that encouraged them to think deeply about the material (Dietz-Uhler & Lanter, 2009). In other words, I want the mean on this exam to look different from the mean in the population that was not exposed to the engaging activity. Similarly, we want the difference between pre- and post-test confidence scores on a critical-thinking module (Dietz-Uhler, 2008) to look different from those same scores in a population that did not participate in the critical-thinking module. We want the probability that we have made an error in our assumptions about the population to be very small. In fact, it is common to set the probability level at .05. Any *p*-value that is less than or equal to .05 is considered to be *statistically significant*.

As you can imagine, there are many different types of inferential statistics, and the inferential statistics you need to make inferences about your data depend on the type of data and the research design. To help you to start thinking about what inferential statistics you need to compute for your project, Table 7.11 shows some sample studies and the types of inferential statistics that were computed.

So now you need to start thinking about the type of inferential statistics you need to compute (or have computed) for your project. In simplistic terms, you need to know the objective of your project to figure out what type of inferential procedure you will need. Table 7.12 lists various project objectives as well as the type of inferential statistic to meet that objective (adapted from www.wakeforestmathtutor.com/test .html).

To learn more about various types of statistics presented in Tables 7.6 and 7.7, consider these easy-to-access and well-written resources:

- *HyperStat Online Statistics Textbook*: http://davidmlane.com/hyperstat

TABLE 7.11
Examples of Studies and Type of Statistics

Study	Basic Question	Type of Data	Inferential Statistics
Phillips, K. E. (2011). A performance-enhanced interactive learning workshop model as a supplement for organic chemistry instruction. *Journal of College Science Teaching, 40*(3), 90–98.	Will a Performance-Enhanced Interactive Learning (PEIL) workshop improve student learning in an organic chemistry class?	Quantitative: four exams and a group presentation	Independent samples *t*-test
Dietz-Uhler, B., & Lanter, R. (2009). Using the four-questions technique to enhance learning. *Teaching of Psychology, 36,* 38–41.	Does engaging in the four-questions activity improve scores on a quiz?	Quantitative: percentage of correct answers on an exam	Analysis of variance (to compare pre- and post-test exam scores for those who engaged in the four-questions activity to those not engaging in it)
Noppe, I., et al. (2007). PowerPoint presentation handouts and college student learning outcomes. *International Journal for the Scholarship of Teaching and Learning, 1*(1). Retrieved April 11, 2008, from http://www.georgia southern.edu/ijsotl	Does supplementing lectures with PowerPoint handouts enhance test-taking performance?	Quantitative: mean and standard deviation test scores	Repeated measures analysis of variance
Bishop-Clark, C., et al. (2007). A quantitative and qualitative investigation of using Alice programming to improve confidence, enjoyment and achievement among non-majors. *Journal of Educational Computing Research, 37*(2), 193–207.	Will students improve their knowledge of programming after a 2.5-week session using Alice?	Quantitative: responses to closed-ended survey questions Qualitative: number of mentions of "improved knowledge" from focus group and essay transcripts	*t*-tests (to compare pre- and post-test data) None
Dietz-Uhler, B., et al. (2005). Formation of and adherence to a self-disclosure norm in an online chat. *CyberPsychology and Behavior, 8,* 114–120.	Does the type of reinforcement students receive in an online discussion foster the number of self-disclosures?	Qualitative: coding of discussion board transcripts	Chi-square analysis of the frequencies of observations for each of the variables
Bishop-Clark, C. (1995). Cognitive style and its effect on the stages of computer programming. *Journal of Research on Computing in Education, 27*(4), 373–386.	Is there is a positive linear correlation between scores attained on a design achievement test and degree of field-independence?	Quantitative: scores on design achievement test and a test of field independence	Correlation

TABLE 7.12 Objectives and Types of Inferential Statistics	
Objective	*Type of Inferential Statistic*
Compare one group to a particular value (e.g., compare responses on a Likert scale to the midpoint of the scale)	One-sample *t*-test
Compare two unpaired groups (e.g., compare exam scores of those completing the four-questions activity to those not completing the four-questions activity)	Independent-samples *t*-test
Compare two paired groups or scores (e.g., compare pre-test attitude scores with post-test attitude scores)	Paired-samples *t*-test
Compare three or more unmatched groups (e.g., compare amount of knowledge expressed in an essay among those who listened to lecture, those who read the text, and those who engaged in an activity)	Independent samples one-way analysis of variance (ANOVA)
Compare three or more matched groups or scores (e.g., comparison of exams one, two, and three)	Repeated measures ANOVA
Measure the association between two variables (e.g., the number of words written in response to a question and exam score)	Correlation
Predict the values of one variable from another (e.g., predict the value of an exam score from the number of times students attended class)	Regression
Compare the frequency of responses in various categories (e.g., the number of self-disclosing statements males and females made)	Chi-square

- *StatSoft Electronic Statistics Textbook*: www.statsoft.com/textbook

---

I already appreciate stats, but I definitely would love to learn more so that I can do it on my own or ask for minimal help. —EVA, SPANISH

Involvement of Students

In the data analysis phase, you can involve students in several ways. First, it is valuable for students to have the opportunity to transfer or transcribe data. Doing so allows them to experience firsthand the details of doing research. Second, students are excellent candidates for coding qualitative data. Like any coders who are blind to the hypothesis of the project, students will need to be trained to code the data. It is a good idea for you and two students to work together and code some of the data to make sure that everyone is on the same page. After that, students can code a portion (e.g., 10%) of the data, and then you can check to make sure they are in agreement (for at least 80%) before proceeding with the remainder of the coding. Third, you might have some students who are statistically savvy and can enter the data into a statistical software program and perform the data analysis.

Analyzing Your Data Worksheet

To help you start thinking about how to prepare your data for analysis, describe what format (e.g., interviews, surveys, essays, exams) your data are currently in and what you will do to transform them into data that can be analyzed (i.e., transcripts, numbers).

Indicate in the box what type of data analysis you will probably perform for each of the variables in your project.

Describe the inferential test(s) you think is (are) most appropriate for your data and your research question.

Are you comfortable analyzing your data? If not, then who will you be able to ask to help you analyze your data?

Regardless of who will analyze your data, how will it be done? Do you need to have data transcribed? Do you need to rely on statistical software? What software might you need?

When will you complete the analysis of your data?

The results of your data analysis may or may not confirm your hypothesis. It is difficult to imagine now what you will do if your results do not confirm your hypothesis, but try to anticipate why this might happen.

Analyzing Your Data: Completed Worksheet

To help you start thinking about how to prepare your data for analysis, describe what format (e.g., interviews, surveys, essays, exams) your data are currently in and what you will do to transform them into data that can be analyzed (i.e., transcripts, numbers).

> The data are in various formats. The quantitative data (attitudes, quiz scores) are on paper. The qualitative data are in the form of transcripts from the focus groups and written essay responses from students.
>
> To transform these data into numerical format, the responses to the survey and the exams need to be entered into a computer program (Excel). The data from the focus groups and essays need to be coded by two people. These will be student assistants.

Indicate in the box what type of data analysis you will probably perform for each of the variables in your project.

> There are three main variables in this study: enjoyment, confidence, and achievement. For the quantitative (survey and exam scores) indicators of these three variables, means and standard deviations are the most appropriate measures of central tendency and variability to compute. For the qualitative indicators (focus groups and essays), percentages of responses in each of the categories will be computed.

Describe the inferential test(s) you think is (are) most appropriate for your data and your research question.

> In this study, we are primarily interested in comparing two matched groups or scores—those on the pre-test and those on the post-test. Therefore, we will compute independent-samples t-tests for the enjoyment, confidence, and achievement items, comparing pre-test with post-test scores.
>
> For the qualitative data, we are mostly interested in using that data for description, or to provide further support for the quantitative results, so we will not compute any inferential statistics on those data.

Are you comfortable analyzing your data? If not, then who will you be able to ask to help you analyze your data?

> One of the researchers in this project is very comfortable analyzing data, so she will take responsibility for performing the statistical analysis. If it turns out to be too complicated, then the researchers are familiar with several social and physical scientists who can assist them.

Regardless of who will analyze your data, how will it be done? Do you need to have data transcribed? Do you need to rely on statistical software? What software might you need?

> Once the data are entered into an Excel worksheet, they will be analyzed. All of the researchers involved are very familiar with Excel, and one of the researchers is very familiar with computing descriptive and inferential statistics in Excel.

When will you complete the analysis of your data?

> We have some practical issues that make us want to complete the analysis soon. Two of the researchers are standing for promotion and tenure soon, and we'd like to have this project published before then. So we will analyze the data immediately.

The results of your data analysis may or may not confirm your hypothesis. It is difficult to imagine now what you will do if your results do not confirm your hypothesis, but try to anticipate why this might happen.

It is possible that our results will not confirm our hypothesis. In fact, prior research in this area has shown that the use of the Alice modules did not improve students' factual knowledge of programming. Regardless, if our hypotheses are not confirmed, we will consider the reasons why. It may be the case that our measures are not sensitive enough to capture the changes in enjoyment, confidence, and achievement. If this is the case, then we probably would try to design better measures and do the study again. It may also be the case that the Alice modules were not long enough, in which case we could spend more time on them.

8

Presenting and Publishing Your Results

AFTER YOU HAVE IDENTIFIED your research question, designed your study, and collected and analyzed your data, you are ready to go public. Chances are good that you have learned something very important about teaching and learning! Chances are also good that you have found ways to improve your own teaching and your students' learning. Such information can and should be shared with your colleagues—those at your own institution and those at others.

You may recall from earlier chapters that, in the early 2000s, the authors team-taught a course, titled "Psychology of the Internet." While team-teaching this course, we developed and systematically evaluated several new and different classroom activities. After collecting some very preliminary data on the success of our activities, we presented our initial findings at a local conference—the Association of University Regional Campuses of Ohio. As the study progressed, we presented our teaching ideas at the Lilly International Conference on College Teaching. We then published two very different papers oriented to different audiences. One of the papers, about our investigation of a single activity within that course (Bishop-Clark & Dietz-Uhler, 2003), was published in the *Journal of Educational Technology Systems*. The other paper reported on four different classroom exercises and their effectiveness (Dietz-Uhler & Bishop-Clark, 2002) and was published in a disciplinary journal (*Psychology Learning and Teaching*) related to teaching and learning. Each of these presentations and papers was the result of a different phase of the project and included distinctly different data. Do not think of your project as having a single endpoint. Instead, think of your SoTL project as telling a story, different parts of which will interest various audiences. Some are interested from the very beginning, when the story is just starting, but we do not know how it will end. Others will be interested only in how the story ends. And some will be most interested in the way the story progresses and the process that unfolds.

I gave three talks in different venues (regional, national, and international conferences). I also submitted two papers for publication. I had to resubmit one of the manuscripts. And after this project, I collaborated with another colleague and we replicated my study. Based on that replication we submitted an article and are writing another one. All in all my SoTL work led to three conference presentations and three publications. —EVA, SPANISH

Importance of Going Public

There is quite a range of what "going public" means. At one end, going public could mean sharing your information with the students in your current class or with your department colleagues. At the other end, going public could mean publishing a scholarly paper in a high-quality, peer-reviewed journal with an international audience. Recall from the first chapter that for work to be categorized as SoTL work, it must result in a formal, peer-reviewed communication that contributes to the larger body of knowledge (Hutchings & Shulman, 1999; Witman & Richlin, 2007). By publishing or presenting your work in the context of what has already been done, you place it among the body of knowledge that exists and move the field as a whole forward.

In her book, *Enhancing Learning Through the Scholarship of Teaching and Learning*, Kathleen McKinney (2007) provides a very interesting discussion and analysis of the meaning of going public and peer review. McKinney suggests that within the academy, the phrase "going public" generally means presentations and publications. However, McKinney points out that going public can also include websites, shared portfolios, performance, and juried shows. She highlights that the value of each of these venues is socially constructed and that such value changes over time. Value is defined by the discipline and by the institution. For instance, in computer science, publication in certain peer-reviewed conference proceedings is considered to be of more value than publication in journals. Similarly, McKinney explains that in some institutions, a course portfolio shared on a website would be a legitimate form of SoTL, but in other institutions it would not. While the academy typically defines "peer-reviewed" as a blind review by several experts in the field, McKinney highlights that there have been many conversations about how to define peer review of SoTL work. Just a few of the issues she outlines include:

- Must peer review be blind?
- Is peer review by an editor sufficient?
- Is peer review solicited by the SoTL researchers legitimate?
- Should peer review for online sharing be different from peer review of traditional print publications?
- Must peers be external to the researcher's campus?

Like our disciplinary research, not all SoTL work is worthy of presentation or publication. Also like disciplinary research, SoTL work can be flawed. The research questions can be too vague, the design flawed,

the data collection process compromised, or analysis of the data incorrect. Not only can various aspects of the process be flawed, but recall the discussion in chapter 2 on the standards and rigor of SoTL work. Chapter 2 stresses that for work to be considered "scholarly," it must be innovative, replicable, well-documented, peer-reviewed, and something that has an impact on the discipline. While they are listed in chapter 2, Glassick and colleagues' (1997) standards of scholarly work are worth repeating:

- Are clear goals of the research articulated?
- Is there demonstrable understanding of the literature?
- Does the scholar articulate methods appropriate for those goals?
- Do the results make a significant contribution to the literature?
- Did the scholar effectively and appropriately communicate the result to the audience?
- Does the scholar critically evaluate the work in a manner that will improve the quality of work?

Not all good SoTL work is "good enough" to be presentable or publishable; however, the fact that you are working through this book means you probably have prepared and implemented a SoTL study worthy of presentation or publication.

Discipline-Specific or General SoTL?

You should consider several issues before deciding how to go public. As we previously discussed, work must be formal, peer-reviewed, and contribute to a larger body of knowledge to be classified as SoTL. Because promotion and tenure decisions are often partially based on contributions within the field, you should seriously consider whether the best outlet for your work will be a presentation or publication within your disciplinary field. Each discipline deals with SoTL work in a different way and each engenders varying levels of respect depending on the discipline. Witman and Richlin (2007) surveyed how various academic disciplines had integrated and used SoTL. The authors reviewed outlets within the discipline for 20 different areas, and they organized their review around four groups: humanities, natural sciences, professions, and social sciences. They conclude that adoption levels of SoTL work range from very high in natural sciences to very low in others. Even within some of the groups, adoption varies. For instance within the humanities, it appears SoTL is well established within the English discipline, but barely established in history.

To decide whether to present or publish within your discipline or within a more general teaching and learning conference or journal, consider the reward system within your discipline, department, and institution. For promotion and tenure in your department, is it important that the work be published in a journal specific to your academic area? Consider whether the topic is of interest to those teaching a variety of disciplines or more interesting to colleagues within your discipline. Consider whether the work is worthy of publication in one of the top-tier SoTL journals such as the *Journal of Excellence in College Teaching* or whether you would have a more interested audience in a discipline-specific journal such as the *Journal of Information Systems Education*. As we illustrated previously, the route you choose is not necessarily exclusive.

I presented my findings at a major conference in my area, APS, because I was already presenting another research project there. My SoTL project was just as popular as my area-specific research and people were excited about the findings. —MICHELLE, PSYCHOLOGY

Presentations

In her chapter on scholarly teaching and the scholarship of teaching, Richlin (2001) includes a flowchart titled a "proposal review decision tree." This is provided as a decision tree used to evaluate proposals for the Lilly Conference on College Teaching. In this flowchart if the project is not complete, the evaluator suggests that the work be presented in poster form. If, on the other hand, the project has been completed and results have been collected, the submission is reviewed as a presentation submission. The point here is not necessarily that incomplete projects should be posters; rather it is to emphasize further that your SoTL work will have various phases and different venues and formats of sharing depending on the phase. Presenting your work at various phases also provides opportunities for valuable feedback. The kinds of feedback you

receive at a SoTL conference where many different disciplines are represented is likely to be very different from the feedback you get from colleagues within your discipline.

A wide range of opportunities falls loosely into the category of "presentations." Presentations range from a departmental brown-bag lunch to presentation at a national conference. For some conferences, a full paper must be submitted before a presentation is accepted, and the full paper is then published in proceedings. As we said previously, within some disciplines, publication in peer-reviewed conference proceedings is more prestigious than publication in certain journals.

On-Campus Presentations

If you have learned something that you find exciting and interesting, share it! SoTL work has the benefit not only of contributing to a body of knowledge but also of improving your particular and unique classroom and perhaps your institution. Your enthusiasm, energy, and interest are likely to spark interest and energy with your colleagues. And it is likely to be especially interesting to your colleagues since you may have collected the data from your student body—the students you and your colleagues work with daily. Sharing your work in a less formal setting, while not categorized as SoTL, is important. One of the first places you should consider sharing your work is within your department or institution. Unlike your disciplinary work, which is often interesting to only a handful of experts on your campus, SoTL work often has much broader application and appeal. A department brown-bag lunch or a campus seminar may be an appropriate first outlet. Our campus has a Center for Teaching and Learning, which sponsors lunches approximately every three weeks on various teaching and learning issues. We have been asked to present at these sessions, but we have also approached the directors of the center and offered a session related to our particular project. The conversation we have at these sessions is engaging and interesting and often gives us ideas for future directions.

Posters

Many SoTL conferences and disciplinary conferences have poster sessions for work that is interesting and relevant but may not be ready for formal presentation or publication. One of the premier SoTL conferences, the Lilly International Conference on College

Teaching, has four different presentation formats. One of those formats is an "interactive poster session." Having participated in several interactive poster sessions, we have often included a professionally created poster (often created via PowerPoint), a laptop with possible illustrations and video clips, and when appropriate, pictures and other objects that help tell the story of our SoTL project. Poster sessions generally provide an opportunity to discuss work in early stages. Posters often have the same sections as papers: author's names, introduction, literature, method, format, results, interpretation, acknowledgments, and references, but do so in a much abbreviated way. As a rule of thumb, when creating posters, use less text and more graphics and pictures. The Lilly Conference even identifies and gives awards for the best poster. The evaluation form for the Lilly Conference can be found at: www.units.muohio.edu/lillycon/guide lines/poster_rubric.pdf. Consider posters when your work may not be ready for a more formal presentation or when you would find value in one-on-one conversation.

State and Regional Conferences

Almost every year, we present some aspect of our SoTL work at a local Association for University Regional Campuses of Ohio (AURCO) conference. Each year, we are no more than a five-hour drive from this conference and our own campus occasionally hosts the conference. The conference only requires that an abstract be submitted for a presentation and we often present the early stages of a SoTL project. In fact, we presented one chapter of this workbook at an AURCO conference while we were in the process of developing it. Look for local, state, and regional conferences that may be appropriate in your area; examples appear in Table 8.1.

National and International Conferences

Not only should you consider local, state, and regional conferences, but national and international confer-

ences as well. Again, consider disciplinary and general SoTL conferences. Many disciplines have conferences devoted to SoTL work. For instance, within the field of computer science, there is a special interest group in computer science education. Each year, this group has an international conference focused on education that follows its technical symposium. This conference attracts thousands of participants from around the world. Full papers are published in the proceedings, which are considered one of the best outlets for finding the latest work in computer science education. The Lilly Conference on College Teaching is in its 30th year. Our institution, Miami University, hosts this international conference each November. Four national Lilly conferences have emerged in various parts of the country (typically north, south, east, and west). Table 8.2 provides a sampling of SoTL conferences and their corresponding websites. A more complete list appears in Appendix A.

Scientific conference presentations are shorter, denser, and usually more technical than those given at SoTL conferences. SoTL presentations often are given more time than those at scientific conferences, allowing a pace more conducive to reflection and making connections among disciplines. Extended or meaningful discussion is rare in scientific conferences; whereas SoTL conferences often encourage and provide prompts for back-and-forth discussion among attendees. And SoTL presentations usually have an audience from a diverse background so there is more interdisciplinary and integrative thinking and discussions. —ALAN, ZOOLOGY

Tips for Presentations

Most of us have presented at a variety of different venues and are familiar with our disciplinary conferences and their norms. Each teaching and learning confer-

TABLE 8.1
Examples of State and Regional Conferences
Annual Midwest Conference on the Scholarship of Teaching and Learning: www.iusb.edu/%7Eucet/sotl.shtml
EDUCAUSE Midwest Regional Conference: www.educause.edu/MWRC11

TABLE 8.2
Examples of SoTL Conferences

International Society for the Scholarship of Teaching and Learning Annual Conference:
issotl11.indiana.edu/index.html

Lilly International Conference on College Teaching:
www.units.muohio.edu/lillycon/

Lilly National Conferences on College and University Teaching:
http://lillyconferences.com/

The SoTL Commons: A Conference for the Scholarship of Teaching and Learning:
http://academics.georgiasouthern.edu/ijsotl/conference/2011/

International Conference on College Teaching and Learning:
www.teachlearn.org/

---

ence has its own flavor and it is important to match your presentation to the culture of the conference. Talk to some of your colleagues about the norms at some of the more popular SoTL conferences. Some are more formal, whereas others prefer more hands-on and active exercises. Table 8.3 summarizes some tips for presentations.

Publications

Local

Just as the first place we suggested you consider presenting your SoTL work is within your institution, you should also explore internal options for presenting your SoTL work in written form. For instance, our campus sends a monthly newsletter (www.mid.muohio.edu/ctl/newsletter.cfm) to campus faculty and staff from the same organization that sponsors the brown-bag lunches. The newsletter announces upcoming events, describes the successes of the center, and shares some of the work our campus colleagues are doing in teaching and learning.

Web Postings

While web postings are not a traditionally accepted means of publishing, they are certainly one way to make work known to a broader audience. In fact, one could argue that a well-designed and well-placed web posting could be more effective in sharing the results of your SoTL project than a peer-reviewed journal article. In her book, *Enhancing Learning Through the*

TABLE 8.3
Tips for Presentations

- Consider whether to go local, regional, national, or international.
- Find a good fit between your presentation and the conference.
- Find a good fit between your message and the delivery type: posters, papers, panels, roundtables.
- Have colleagues critique your presentation before the conference.
- Choose a title that clearly reflects the content.
- Review the websites for creating and delivering effective presentations.
- Consider your audience and its interests.
- If creating a poster, use a predefined poster template (such as PowerPoint).
- When presenting, take a deep breath, watch your pace, make eye contact, and allow time for questions and comments.

Scholarship of Teaching and Learning, Kathleen McKinney (2007) suggests looking into whether your particular campus or disciplinary association has a repository of SoTL work. She directs readers to several repositories of information, including Carnegie Foundation Gallery of Teaching (http://gallery.carnegie foundation.org/), Georgetown University Visual Knowledge Project (http://crossroads.georgetown.edu/vkp/), and the Indiana University Peer Review Project (www.indiana.edu/~deanfac/portfolio/). Each of these sites (as well as many others) has its own style and flavor. Be sure to search for established SoTL websites within your particular discipline.

Newsletters, Editorials, Monographs, and Book Chapters

In addition to local publications and web postings, many journals have outlets for articles about research that is not ready for publication as a full-fledged journal article but may be of interest to a broader community. Weimer (2006) does a good job of highlighting some of these other areas for publication. She states that disciplinary journals often have their own special sections that publish manuscripts outside full-fledged journal articles. The *Journal of Nursing Education* includes "briefs," which are small-scale studies, educational innovations, editorial comments, and opinion pieces. The *Academy of Management Learning and Education* publishes essays, dialogues, and interviews about current and future trends in teaching, learning, and management education. *Teaching of Psychology* includes pieces on the impact of computer technology on the teaching of psychology. And many disciplinary journals, including the *Journal of Chemical Education*, include a "teaching tips" section with practical advice for everyday teaching. In addition to outlets within disciplinary journal articles, several editors have published edited collections of SoTL work. In her book, *Opening Lines: Approaches to the Scholarship of Teaching and Learning*, Pat Hutchings (2000) published a series of eight case studies. Each of these case studies represents an effort by one of the Carnegie Scholars during a particular year. Hutchings's goal for including the variety of studies is to illustrate that there are many methods of and approaches to SoTL. Similarly, we were recently invited to write a chapter on our SoTL learning community for a book on SoTL learning communities. Clearly, not all faculty members are Carnegie Scholars or experts in SoTL, and opportunities may not be as readily available to us as to the Carnegie Scholars Hutchings writes about, but the point of this particular section and the previous one is to encourage you to think beyond a traditional journal article as a potential outlet for publication.

Journals

Certainly the most traditional and accepted form of sharing new knowledge within the academy is in the form of peer-reviewed journal publications. Typically, multiple experts in the field blind-review manuscripts. The reviewers' expertise may be in the methodology used or the topic at hand. Perhaps the single most important aspect of success (outside of a good study) is finding the right fit between your manuscript and the kind of papers a particular journal publishes. Each journal has a notes to author section and many give the rubric reviewers use when evaluating papers. Rubrics may contain some or all of the following sections: appropriateness for the journal, importance of the topic, quality of writing, quality of content, literature review, theoretical framework, research methods, results, discussion, and conclusion.

Like conferences, you have to decide whether to publish your work in a discipline-specific or general SoTL journal. Appendix C includes a complete list of discipline-focused SoTL journals, and the number of such journals continues to grow. Journals range from the *Journal of Accounting Education* to *Research in Drama Education* to *Physics Education*. Virtually all disciplines have multiple journals appropriate for SoTL research. In addition to discipline-specific journals, other journals focus on the scholarship of teaching and learning in a more general way. Appendix B includes a complete list of such journals. Perusing this list shows many such journals, including one published by Miami University—the *Journal on Excellence in College Teaching*. This journal publishes papers that demonstrate excellence in research, integration, innovation, or inspiration. The papers that appear in the journal may be specific to a discipline or they may be interdisciplinary. The journal publishes two to four times a year, with periodic issues focusing on special topics. The editorial staff screens submissions to this journal first. Papers deemed appropriate for the journal are then sent to two expert reviewers in teaching scholarship. The journal accepts 20% of its submissions. However 50% of papers are immediately returned without being sent out for review for three reasons: there is no evidence of student learning (simply a report of what students liked), there are no baseline data for comparison, or the paper simply does not add anything new to the knowledge base.

Like many disciplinary journals, certain measures can be used to evaluate the quality of the journal. Some universities want to see "impact factors" and "acceptance rates" of journals, so those outside the discipline can make some assessment of the quality of journals. This may be even more important if you are publishing in a journal with which your department is unfamiliar. Impact factor is a rough measure of the number of citations received per paper published in that journal in the two preceding years. The higher the impact factor, the more influential and important the journal is deemed to be. While there are plenty of criticisms of the validity of impact factors, among certain fields they are used for credibility. Acceptance rates are a second measure sometimes used to evaluate quality. Acceptance rates vary tremendously from one journal to the next. While not complete, McLeod, Tulloch, Ritter, and Kent (2005) provide the impact factors of some SoTL journals. Editors of certain journals may also be able to provide impact factors and acceptance rates.

Tips for Publication

The single most important aspect of publishing your SoTL work is to get the manuscript written! In the SoTL learning communities we have led, all of the participants in our group have completed SoTL projects with interesting results. Everyone in our learning community presented his or her work in either a disciplinary or SoTL conference. Unfortunately, only about one-third of participants wrote a paper and submitted it for publication. Many of the remaining two-thirds are sitting on a data set with results that are interesting and publishable. Given all the demands placed on faculty members, making the time to draft a manuscript is difficult. We have used multiple strategies for finding such time. We have blocked off one day a week to write. We have used one hour every day to work on a manuscript. We have a colleague who occasionally leaves the office a few hours early to draft papers at a coffee shop; the background noise helps him concentrate. We have another colleague who prefers complete solitude. She works at home and disconnects her phones and Internet. Some people use "writing buddies"; others create artificial deadlines. Identify the method that works for you. If you have taken the time to work through this book, complete the process by sharing what you have learned! It is critical to the growth of the field, and in some cases it is critical to your own quest for promotion and tenure.

***

Confidence was my issue in getting the manuscript off my desk. I just wasn't sure I had given enough information. I finally wrote every day (Mon–Fri) for about three weeks in getting this through the first draft. Once I had the draft finished, I ended up letting it sit on my desk for some time. I ran into a colleague who asked how I was doing with the paper and I admitted it was sitting on my desk. My colleague made me accountable by having me e-mail her when I finally sent my paper to Clinical Simulation in Nursing, *where after several revisions it was published.* —DEBBIE, NURSING

***

Perhaps the second most important aspect of publishing your work is finding a good fit between your manuscript and the publication outlet. Maurer (2011) calls this "understanding your audience." He further explains that for the *International Journal for the Scholarship of Teaching and Learning*, since it is interdisciplinary, a manuscript must have implications that extend beyond the scope of any particular discipline. He explains that for international journals, it is important to present findings in a global context. For your manuscript, ask whether the readers of this particular journal would be interested in your work. Is this manuscript appropriate for the focus of this particular journal? Journals have "guidelines for authors" or "call for papers" that detail the kinds of papers the journal publishes. Review these guidelines carefully.

Third, while it may seem trivial, several editors comment about the high number of submitted manuscripts that do not conform to the specifications for submission (Maurer, 2011; McKinney, 2007). Be sure you format appropriately, follow guidelines for the length of submission, carefully review and edit your document, use the appropriate style, and write in a clear and concise manner. Stefani (2011) outlines the characteristics of a high-quality SoTL article for the *International Journal of the Scholarship of Teaching and Learning* and points out that these characteristics are similar to disciplinary journals. Specifically, she suggests:

- An introduction to the nature of the study
- A literature review that puts your study in the context of prior work
- A clear and concise description of the hypothesis and research plan
- A well-articulated research design
- Appropriate interpretation of results
- Sufficient information for other researchers to replicate and duplicate the study

Table 8.4 provides a few tips to review as you write your manuscript.

Student Involvement

Early in her career, Cathy Bishop-Clark authored a paper that included the voice of the student and the voice of the teacher. The topic was a freshman honors course on computers and society. Because the course was unique at the time, she drafted a manuscript about it. The student contributed to writing the journal article by drafting her perspective of the course and its activities. She reflected on her learning, on which activities helped her gain insight into the topic at hand, and on which activities did not help with her learning. The student's voice was interesting and powerful.

Similarly, we have engaged in presentations in which the audience heard two voices: the participants (students) and the facilitator (teacher). As we have mentioned throughout the book, we have led multiple SoTL learning communities. We presented the challenges and successes of leading these learning communities at a regional and a national conference, and during the presentation, we traded stories (some from the student and some from the teacher). Those in the audience very much enjoyed hearing both points of view.

Not only can students be copresenters and coauthors, but they are often highly proficient in designing websites, drafting newsletters, and exploring the more innovative ways to share SoTL work.

TABLE 8.4
Tips for Writing the Manuscript

- Find a good fit between your manuscript and the outlet (local publications, web posting, newsletters, journal articles, etc.).
- Consider the audience of the paper as you draft your manuscript.
- Get feedback from colleagues.
- After writing the manuscript, let it rest a few days and then revisit it.
- Embed your work in the context of existing literature and be sure the literature is current.
- Write a complete, concise, and engaging abstract. Many readers will determine whether to continue reading based solely on the abstract.
- Consider using stories of incidents that occurred during your SoTL project to illustrate main points or provide additional insight to numeric results.
- Check and recheck that your manuscript is error-free, easy to read and understand, and concise.
- Never submit a manuscript to more than one journal at the same time.
- Carefully follow guidelines for page length and style.

Presenting and Publishing Your SoTL Project: Worksheet

What are the topic, purpose, and potential audience for your SoTL project?

Topic	
Purpose	
Potential Audience	

Identify whether local outlets (within your institution) are available for you to share your work. For instance, is your department, division, or a learning community interested in your findings?

Identify two potential conferences for your SoTL project. For each conference, identify important dates and specify whether the conference is regional, national, or international.

Conference and Conference Description	Local, Regional, National, or International	Date of Conference and Deadline for Submissions

Identify one or two potential discipline-specific journals. Give some evaluation of the quality of the journal.

Journal	Evaluation of Quality

Identify one or two potential journals that are general pedagogical journals and give some evaluation of the quality of the journal(s).

Journal	Evaluation of Quality

Identify three colleagues who can review drafts of your paper.

Give yourself a deadline for completing your manuscript.

Presenting and Publishing Your SoTL Project: Completed Worksheet

What are the topic, purpose, and potential audience for your SoTL project?

Topic	Changes in students' confidence, enjoyment, and knowledge of programming after a 2.5-week session using a new programming language.
Purpose	To determine whether the department should adopt a new programming language for a liberal education course and to build the knowledge base on the effectiveness of this new educational tool.
Potential Audience	Computer science and information technology educators, the department, faculty teaching other general education courses.

Identify whether local outlets (within your institution) are available for you to share your work. For instance, is your department, division, or a learning community interested in your findings?

Department, possibly a session for our Center for Teaching and Learning

Identify two potential conferences for your SoTL project. For each conference, identify important dates and specify whether the conference is regional, national, or international.

Conference and Conference Description	Local, Regional, National, or International	Date of Conference and Deadline for Submissions
Consortium for Computing Sciences in Colleges	Regional	September conference with a March submission deadline
Special Interest Group Computer Science Education	National	March conference with a summer submission deadline

Identify one or two potential discipline-specific journals. Give some evaluation of the quality of the journal.

Journal	Evaluation of Quality
Journal of Educational Computing Research	15% acceptance rate; impact factor of .13; 1,000–2,000 subscribers
Journal of Research on Computing in Education	28% acceptance rate; 2,250–3,000 subscribers

Identify one or two potential journals that are general pedagogical journals and give some evaluation of the quality of the journal(s).

Journal	Evaluation of Quality
International Journal of Teaching and Learning in Higher Education	This is an electronic journal; 5,363 people from 114 countries are notified of new issues

Identify three colleagues who can review drafts of your paper.

> Department chair, department colleague, English department colleague

Give yourself a deadline for completing your manuscript.

> Three months from today

9

Challenges of and Solutions for Doing Research on Teaching and Learning

IN THIS FINAL CHAPTER we take a step back from the process of designing and implementing a SoTL project and consider in more detail some of the broader challenges and solutions of engaging in SoTL. We recognize that there are different levels of engagement in SoTL, ranging from doing a SoTL project every now and then to pursuing a career devoted mostly to SoTL. Your reasons for wanting to do a SoTL project and your expected level of SoTL activity are worth spending some time thinking about, particularly if you are an untenured faculty member. As we shared in the first chapter, our own levels of SoTL interest and activity differ. Cathy has made a career of SoTL by interweaving her teaching, service, and research interests and obligations. She was successfully tenured and promoted (eventually to full professor) based almost entirely on SoTL as her primary research. Beth devoted her early research career entirely to disciplinary research. Once tenured and promoted to associate professor, she developed an interest in SoTL but still engaged in some disciplinary research. Her promotion to full professor was based on a research record consisting of a mix between SoTL and disciplinary research. Although our institution values excellent teaching, until fairly recently, it did not especially value SoTL as a form of scholarship. Your level of engagement in SoTL will likely depend on where you are in your career, the reputation of SoTL at your institution, and the level of departmental and institutional support for SoTL.

The goal of this chapter is to help you figure out your level of engagement in SoTL by acquainting you with the literature on the value and reputation of SoTL, the reward structure of SoTL, practical challenges of doing SoTL, and practices that departments and institutions can adopt to make SoTL a better-supported scholarly endeavor. We conclude the chapter and the book the way we began—with a story. Our final story is about a nursing faculty member who, using the five-step process outlined in this book, turned her SoTL idea into a $2 million grant in just over two years.

Value and Reputation of SoTL

In the first chapter we mentioned that, historically, SoTL has not been particularly valued in higher education, prompting Boyer (1990) to promote the idea that all four forms of scholarship (integration, discovery, application, and teaching) should be valued equally. At most institutions of higher education, these four forms of scholarship are not at parity. The scholarship of discovery continues to be more privileged than the other three types of scholarship (Elton, 2008; Gurm, 2009). For example, Braxton, Luckey, and Helland (2002), in a survey of close to 1,500 faculty at five different institutions, found that 75% of faculty had not listed any SoTL publications on their CVs in the previous five years. Huber (2004) suggests that, although there is evidence that the value placed on SoTL in higher education has improved in the last 30 years, the rate of change has been uneven, with some institutions changing more rapidly than others. Similarly, Gallos (2008) indicates that there are still limitations in the field of SoTL. These limitations include SoTL:

- that is too disparate;
- is still focused on teaching practices;
- lacks research on such topics as learning styles and differences in types of students;
- needs interdisciplinary research;
- does not fully contribute to the knowledge base on teaching and learning;
- does not measure student learning and skills that will matter in the future;
- is largely unsupported by the reward system at most institutions; and
- lacks a common conceptualization.

An interesting paradox is that all institutions of higher education value excellent teaching, but often fail to demonstrate its value and importance (McKinney, 2007; Pan, 2009; Shapiro, 2006). This is especially the case at small liberal arts colleges and community colleges, where often any form of scholarship is not valued (e.g., Kelley-Kleese, 2003; Tinberg, Duffy, & Mino, 2007). There are multiple reasons why SoTL's value and reputation in higher education is uneven. One may be how we talk about SoTL. Some people value SoTL and believe it should be treated the same as disciplinary scholarship, whereas others see SoTL as a form of "excellent teaching" rather than scholarship (Bernstein, 2010). Another reason may be how we conceptualize and define "scholarship." Some people think of scholarship as being strictly disciplinary and of enough intellectual rigor to be published in disciplinary research journals (Bernstein, 2010). Of course, one can easily make a case that much SoTL research is of the same intellectual rigor as disciplinary research. Maintaining these different conceptualizations of scholarship and publishing in different (disciplinary versus SoTL) journals only magnifies the barriers between the scholarship of teaching and the scholarship of discovery (Gurung & Schwartz, 2010).

How are the four forms of scholarship valued at your institution? In particular, how much (or how little) is SoTL valued in your department, division, and institution? Kathleen McKinney (2007), a notable figure in the SoTL field, offers common concerns and reasons for resistance to SoTL that she has heard over the years. Before starting your own SoTL agenda, consider where your institution is with regard to these attitudes toward and conceptualizations of SoTL:

- SoTL is not really research or scholarship.
- SoTL is poor-quality research or scholarship.
- SoTL results cannot be generalized.
- SoTL should not count as research or scholarship, only as teaching.
- Many faculty/staff lack the expertise to do SoTL.
- There are insufficient resources (money, time, help) to do SoTL.
- SoTL work will not be adequately valued and rewarded on campus.
- SoTL work will not be adequately valued and rewarded in the discipline.
- SoTL will take away from real research and scholarship in the field.
- There is no network of SoTL scholars on campus. (pp. 20–21)

I was worried about the value my department would put on my SoTL work. My concern was that I would spend valuable research time and resources on activities that, although I valued [them], my department would not consider a good investment.
—MICHELLE, PSYCHOLOGY

For many of the reasons we consider next, it is worthwhile to ponder these issues and, if necessary, talk to some colleagues to get their sense of the value of SoTL in your department and at your institution. As we mentioned earlier, our institution is clearly moving in the direction of valuing SoTL as well as the scholarship of service. It goes without saying that we are thrilled with this change as it has allowed us the freedom to share our SoTL experiences and excitement. We have received encouragement and strong support in conducting workshops on SoTL, facilitating SoTL faculty learning communities, and collaborating with junior and peer-level colleagues on SoTL projects.

Reward Structure of SoTL

Why does it matter whether SoTL is valued at your institution? If you love and value SoTL, isn't that good enough? Obviously, the answer to this second question is no. How SoTL is valued at your institution has implications for promotion and tenure, merit raises, advancement opportunities, and interactions with your colleagues. And as we indicated previously, valuing and rewarding SoTL are not necessarily the same. Just because your institution values the pursuit of excellent teaching does not necessarily mean it values the scholarship of teaching. There is some evidence, though, that the climate at many institutions is changing. Hutchings (2010) suggests that research on teaching and learning is slowly making its way into institutional practices and policies concerning rewards for faculty. The Association of American Colleges and Universities (AAC&U) (2008), in *Our Students' Best Work: A Framework for Accountability Worthy of Our Mission*, states, "Campus reward systems should incorporate the importance of faculty members' intellectual and professional leadership in both assessment and educational improvement." (p. 12). While assessment is not the same as SoTL, rewarding assessment of student learning outcomes is likely to pave the way for rewarding SoTL.

One of the most frequently voiced concerns we have heard when we conduct workshops is the issue of promotion and tenure, and for good reason. Tenure-track faculty are mentored and strongly encouraged to become competent teachers while at the same time becoming excellent disciplinary scholars (Shapiro, 2006). As several authors (e.g., Weimer, 2006; Witman & Richlin, 2007) have observed, SoTL generally does not count as productive and credible scholarship. In fact, some faculty members fear that a commitment to SoTL will jeopardize their chances for promotion and tenure (Gelmon & Agre-Kippenhan, 2002). Among other things, such fear is likely to lead many faculty members to pass up opportunities to engage in SoTL (Shapiro, 2006).

I didn't have huge concerns about promotion and tenure (P&T) on my campus. I had heard from successful professors who had "made a career out of SoTL work." This statement was very powerful to me. Also, since I was able to pull in a discipli-

nary focus, I felt that I was "covered." Fortunately, in my discipline, SoTL work is not unheard of.
—Brooke, Nursing

Can a faculty member get promoted and tenured with a CV that is dominated by the scholarship of teaching? Weimer (2006) suggests looking at the CVs of full professors at one's institution. How much SoTL work appears? Were they promoted on the basis of their SoTL research? How about newly tenured and promoted associate professors? How much SoTL work appears on their CVs? Answers to these questions probably will give you some clues about the likelihood of being tenured and promoted with SoTL work in your dossier.

What are the challenges of being promoted and tenured based on SoTL work? First, consider the task of the P&T committee. One of its roles is to discern the distinction of your scholarship and your teaching and service (Huber, 2004). P&T committees have experience evaluating teaching, service, and disciplinary research, but most likely have far less experience evaluating SoTL. If they are unfamiliar with SoTL, how will they be able to evaluate the SoTL work in a P&T dossier? Second, most institutions require external reviews of scholarship for P&T. Are there SoTL scholars in your discipline who can evaluate your SoTL work? If not, will your institution give weight to the evaluation of a reviewer outside your discipline? Weimer (2008) describes three problems when disciplinary colleagues attempt to evaluate SoTL. Discipline-based colleagues probably do not have sophisticated knowledge of pedagogical literature or much knowledge of the methodology used in SoTL work. Finally, many forms of SoTL are unique and often diverge from the purposes of disciplinary research, making it difficult for non–SoTL experts to evaluate SoTL work.

My concern was with others outside my discipline who may not understand that SoTL work has been an integral part of nursing education. They might not think it offered "enough scholarship for promotion and tenure." —Debbie, Nursing

As you think about your level of interest and involvement in SoTL, it is worthwhile to consider all of the issues raised previously. Although we have devoted much discussion in this chapter to the possible disadvantages of an academic career devoted to SoTL, especially when a faculty member is not tenured, we hope you will not be discouraged. As we discussed in chapter 1, there are many positive reasons for faculty members and students to engage in SoTL. And doing SoTL can be rewarding even in institutions largely devoted to research. In *Balancing Acts*, Huber (2004) presents four case studies of scholars who were successfully promoted and tenured and had strong records of SoTL work. All four scholars faced challenges but found ways to be rewarded for their SoTL work.

Challenges of Doing SoTL

In addition to promotion and tenure, there are some practical issues to consider before starting a SoTL project. We discussed many of these in chapter 3, but for the moment, let's consider a few of them. One of the first issues to consider when embarking on any new project is *time*. Do you have the time to read the literature related to your SoTL interests? Do you have the time to learn new or different methods of conducting the research? Do you have the time to carry out the project, examine the results, and present or publish your findings? A second issue is your current level of *scholarly expertise*. Do you have the tools necessary to conduct a SoTL project from start to finish? If you do not have all of the skills you will need, do you have colleagues with whom you can collaborate? A third issue is *assistance*. Do you have graduate or undergraduate assistants who can help you?

> *I think that I struggled in two ways. One was that I felt "behind" in the process, as compared to peers who were beginning to do SoTL work. I felt that my lack of research experience on a larger scale was detrimental. In addition, I think that I spent a lot of time finding the right topic for my first project. This was a little frustrating because I continued to feel behind. However, I think that this was a good thing in the end. My original SoTL project is in its third year now. The topic has served me well!* —BROOKE, NURSING

There are also larger-scale challenges to consider. The first is the issue of rigor and excellence we discussed in chapter 1. As Hutchings and Shulman (1999) indicate, it is one thing to engage in SoTL because we think our students will benefit from it, and another to engage in SoTL that meets the standards of rigorous and excellent scholarship. Another challenge involved in doing SoTL is the issue of support that we mentioned previously. Witman and Richlin (2007) make the case that many faculty do not engage in SoTL because of the absence of support for doing so. Bernstein (2010) offers another, quite interesting challenge. He suggests that few faculty members can *do* the scholarship of teaching for a number of reasons. First, faculty members with the greatest teaching obligations have fewer hours to devote to SoTL. Second, the disciplinary training of many faculty does not allow for an easy transition from disciplinary research to SoTL. He argues that the social sciences can make the transition most easily, but those in the natural sciences and humanities have a bigger leap to make. Another challenge is the potential isolation faculty engaged in SoTL face from those engaged in disciplinary research (McKinney, 2002). Tinberg and colleagues (2007) refer to this as "pedagogical solitude." Not being able to talk about your research or engage in intellectual conversations about it can make it less enjoyable.

> *My challenges were mostly from within myself. Not being trained as a researcher, some of the process (statistics) and design were overwhelming. Having support from the SoTL mentors and the other members of the group was imperative to my success.* —DEBBIE, NURSING

In a study of faculty members who received small grants to support a SoTL project, McKinney and Jarvis (2009) found several reasons why faculty had difficulty applying the results of their SoTL projects. These included not enough time for research, insufficient funding, their own time management skills, and lack of collaboration that would facilitate application. These are all likely challenges to those trying to engage in a SoTL project, let alone trying to apply the findings to the classroom or beyond.

My project was based on three sections of a course where I was not the instructor. It took me a lot of time to train, inform the instructor and a grader, and to make sure every part of the project was conducted successfully. Sometimes participants did not come to class or did not submit an assignment. The experience was very rewarding for all of us at the end but it required a lot of organization involving different people. —EVA, SPANISH

Solutions

We've identified several challenges, ranging from practical issues to larger, institutional ones. These are all important, realistic issues to consider as you begin to develop your SoTL project. Some of them may cause you to rethink your decision to start a SoTL project (we hope not), while others may lead you to alter some things you planned to do. But before making any of these decisions, you should examine some solutions to the issues and challenges we've highlighted.

Individual-Level Solutions
At the practical level, Gelmon and Agre-Kippenhan (2002) offer multiple suggestions for navigating P&T. Many of these suggestions focus on faculty whose primary scholarly interests are in SoTL. These include:

- Be mission-driven: Frame work around the mission of the department or institution.
- Anticipate review committee composition: Find out, early on, who will be on your P&T committee, and ask if you can include other members who will be supportive of your SoTL efforts.
- Know the guidelines: Understand the requirements for P&T and write your dossier in a manner that conforms to the standards.
- Create linkages: Clarify the links between your discipline and your work in SoTL.
- Seek strong letters of support: Identify scholars in SoTL who are willing and able to write strong letters of support.
- Match your work to reviewers' expertise: Ask that specific reviewers evaluate specific parts of your SoTL work.

I found it easy to design a good study but difficult to marshal the resources I needed to complete it. Every step seemed a hurdle. First I had to find money to hire students to code the study, then learn how to write a grant application to get the money, then find students with the necessary capability and time to do the work, then find someone who could tell me how to actually negotiate the red tape necessary to hire these assistants, and complete all the bureaucratic steps. Then when the study was completed, I needed help to statistically analyze the data. I still need some advice about how to cast the study into the appropriate format for publishing. The total process was and is quite challenging for someone not trained in social science. —MARY JANE, ENGLISH

Tsang (2010) offers practical recommendations for those interested in SoTL as their primary form of scholarship. She proposes that one pursue SoTL collaboratively, seeking to work with others who share the same goals and interests. It is especially important to build bridges with colleagues more experienced in the discipline. It is also a good idea to forge connections with those in the larger SoTL community, such as participants in and speakers at a SoTL conference or workshop. She also recommends that those interested in pursuing SoTL closely guard their time to reflect, write, and plan SoTL activities. She writes, "Crudely put, two hours spent on a staff meeting with no agenda or definite goals are better spent in critical reflection or in scholarly writing" (p . 5). McKinney and Jarvis (2009) describe the resources that are needed to engage in SoTL, which include funding opportunities for research and for travel to conferences and workshops, resources to create SoTL communities, and availability of local outlets to disseminate results.

Our own individual solutions to navigating P&T were similar. For Cathy, the key was to interweave teaching, service, and research in such a way that one could not exist without the other two. This approach allowed for a coherent package to be presented for P&T as well as a well-organized and streamlined approach to teaching, service, and research responsibilities. For Beth, the key was to combine disciplinary research with SoTL. For example, our research on computer-mediated communication in the classroom was directly related to disciplinary interests, as was our research on the effectiveness of activities in our team-taught Psychology of the Internet course. In both cases, the key was to combine and interweave interests so we were not burning the candle at both ends.

Institutional-Level Solutions

Many of the recommendations that have been proposed in the literature are aimed at a larger-scale, institutional level. We recognize that some readers may not be in the position to instigate institutional-level reforms, but you should be aware of them. Even if you are not in a position to start reforms at your institution, awareness of the possibilities might allow you to plant some seeds. Some of these recommendations include creating *structural elements* of the institution. For example, Shulman (2004) advances the idea of "teaching academies," which include

> a combination of support structures and sanctuaries, that is, places where faculty whose scholarly interests include teaching and learning can find safety, support and even colleagueship for doing good work on the pedagogies of their fields. (p. 9)

He proposes four models of teaching academies. Briefly, these include:

1. Interdisciplinary Center: Includes members from different disciplines who share common interests and ideas for pedagogical research.
2. Aspect of Graduate Education: The goal of this is to prepare doctoral students for pedagogical scholarship.
3. Organized Around Technology: Explores the role of technology in teaching and learning.
4. Distributed: Provides central support but distributes efforts at pedagogical research across departments, programs, etc.

Other recommendations focus on making *cultural changes* at the institutional level. For example, Glassick and colleagues (1997) make a case for "trusting the process," committing to and being confident that institutions will support the range of scholarship and evaluate it using appropriate standards. How is such trust achieved? Glassick et al. (1997) suggest that it occurs via a process that accommodates a range of schol-

arship, maintains standards of quality and rigor, and provides documentation that encourages and creates trust. For such cultural changes to occur, it is important to have champions of SoTL in key university positions (Gurung & Schwartz, 2010; Huber, 2004). But it is also important to build such efforts from the ground up. These may be areas where you can have a voice in instigating change, assuming that your institution needs such change. There are a number of ways to accomplish this. For example, Sperling (2003) suggests:

- Talking the talk: Frequently using language such as "scholarship of teaching and learning," "reflection," and "research."
- Developing a culture that values inquiry but does not expect teachers to have all of the answers. It is important to promote a culture in which taking risks is safe and valued.
- Remembering that it is all about students. SoTL is not necessarily about faculty; it is about students.

Similarly, Kelly-Kleese (2003) recommends a number of practices for institutions trying to create a culture that values SoTL. These include:

1. Define scholarship so that it fits with the mission and purpose of your institution.
2. Promote scholarship among faculty and staff.
3. Support faculty and staff who are interested in engaging in SoTL.
4. Provide opportunities for faculty and staff to pursue SoTL.
5. Share SoTL generated by faculty and staff within the institution and beyond.
6. Reward faculty and staff for engaging in SoTL.
7. Evaluate practices and policies to determine whether they discourage faculty and staff from engaging in SoTL.
8. Commit to a culture that values SoTL.

We contributed to the cultural change at our institution by talking with colleagues about our own SoTL projects. Eventually, our colleagues expressed interest in learning more about SoTL and engaging in their own SoTL projects. Thrilled by this interest, we began to develop and offer workshops on how to do SoTL.

The responses to these workshops were so positive that we started several faculty learning communities where we assisted participants in developing their own SoTL projects from start to finish. At our institution, there is a large cadre of faculty who are engaged in SoTL.

If we heard from administrators or/and we read in university documents about SoTL's impact in our professions, I think faculty would pay more attention to it. Another idea would be to make people like you more visible with your SoTL work and contributions throughout MU. —EVA, SPANISH

A third model includes a *combination of structural and cultural changes.* McConnell (2004) describes how Rockhurst University met the challenge of rewarding SoTL in P&T decisions. Members of the university formed a "Campus Inquiry Group" to explore the issues involved in making SoTL more public and including it in P&T decisions. Eventually the Campus Inquiry Group adopted a statement about the importance of SoTL, which the university ultimately accepted and applied to all future P&T decisions. McConnell (2004) suggests that three factors contributed to the success of securing support for SoTL in P&T decisions at Rockhurst. These include formation of a committee whose members were well-respected and experienced, having a supportive administration, and having champions of SoTL in key positions as well as connecting to the larger SoTL community outside their university. McKinney (2002) argues that a cultural shift needs to include changes in how we define and view the roles of those heavily involved in teaching and learning. She maintains that just as we have an obligation and responsibility to be scholarly in our disciplines, so, too, do we have a responsibility to be scholarly in our approach to teaching. How does such a cultural change occur? She suggests it will involve structural changes, such as developing a model that supports doing SoTL and rewarding it properly. Similarly, Huber and Hutchings (2005) advocate a "teaching commons" that provides the intellectual, physical, and social space for SoTL collaborations.

Make it transparent that SoTL research will be considered on par with area-specific research. I know

that my school values excellence in teaching; the opinion on research on teaching is not as obvious. There were considerable conflicting opinions and it would be nice if the "official" opinion was clear. —MICHELLE, PSYCHOLOGY

Involving Students

In addition to thinking about the challenges faculty face when conducting SoTL projects, it is also wise to consider the challenges that student collaborators or assistants might have. These are similar to the challenges faculty face and can include practical and larger-scale career issues. Challenges at the practical level include time—do students have the time to commit fully to assisting or collaborating in a SoTL project? Time issues that students will need to consider include time away from classes, extracurricular activities, work, family, and friends. A related issue that students should be mindful of is their grade point average. Will engaging in SoTL take time away from their classes in a manner that will have a negative impact on their performance? A student's level of expertise or knowledge in the particular SoTL topic might also be an issue. If the student has to spend time and energy learning about a new area, he or she needs to decide whether this is a wise and productive use of their time.

At the career level, students need to consider whether engaging in SoTL will help or hinder their future career plans. One issue is whether engaging in SoTL prevents or discourages students from pursuing research in their major, although you should note that McKinney (2009) found that students involved in SoTL reported being more connected to their discipline. But students need to consider the value of engaging in SoTL when completing a job application or an application to graduate school. Similarly, students need to consider whether acquiring knowledge about SoTL and the particular SoTL topic being investigated is important to their career goals, or whether that time would be better spent acquiring knowledge and skills more relevant to their career plans.

Conclusion

We conclude this chapter and the book the way we began—with a story. For each of us, SoTL has been one of the most important and interesting threads of our career. It has informed our teaching, influenced departmental policy, been the foundation for winning various teaching awards, and energized our careers. SoTL has led to some unique opportunities, including working with others outside our discipline. Our work has changed the way we think about scholarship, which has broadened and genuinely embraced Boyer's (1990) definition of *the scholarship of teaching*. SoTL has allowed us to learn from scholars and build on the existing body of SoTL knowledge. Not only has SoTL changed the way we define scholarship, it also has had a powerful influence on the way we teach. Our teaching and scholarship are woven together to the point where it seems unnatural to separate them.

The final story we share is not our story but the story of one of the participants (Brooke Flinders) in our SoTL faculty learning committee. Brooke began as a SoTL novice with several vague and ill-defined ideas for her project. In the beginning she wanted to do a SoTL project on either English as a Second Language with nursing students or some aspect of service learning with nursing students. Recall that one of the first steps in the process is to move from a vague idea to a clear, well-defined question. She worked through the five-step process we have outlined in the book by completing the same worksheets we've included at the end of each chapter. In just over two years, she turned her ill-defined SoTL idea into a $2 million project funded by the U.S. Department of Health and Human Services, Office of Adolescent Health.

A Success Story: Brooke Flinders

Although I didn't have a name for it at the time, I would guess that one of my first exposures to the Scholarship of Teaching and Learning occurred when Dr. Cathy Bishop-Clark was my professor, almost 18 years ago. I distinctly remember her course and her interest in the success of her students. Even now, I recall her connectedness to me as an undergraduate.

My specialty, in advanced practice nursing, is in midwifery and women's health; I am a confident, experienced nurse. I began my career in higher education as an adjunct clinical faculty member. For the first year I taught only in the hospital setting, on obstetrical rotations. I was completely at ease in teaching clinicals. I trusted my assessment skills and my ability to

teach my students in a nonthreatening way so they could learn as much as possible.

When I began teaching two years later as a tenure-track faculty member, I found myself in the uncomfortable role of novice again. I knew that I could teach because I was an excellent student and because I had spent so many years educating my patients and their families. What I didn't know, though, was how to *do* tenure track. I had never heard of a dossier, to be honest, and the concept of the teaching-scholarship-service triad was brand new to me as well. I am fortunate to teach at a university that is rich in support and resources, but I found that the responsibility to connect with the resources was my own. Even though it would have been easy to consume myself with the minute details that come with developing course syllabi and exams, I was exposed to a bigger picture very early on.

I was involved with our Center for Excellence in Learning and Teaching and University Assessment from my first year as a visiting professor. I came to understand the importance of having interdisciplinary (and interdepartmental) connections from the very beginning of my academic career. I heard Dr. Bishop-Clark and Dr. Dietz-Uhler speak at a faculty-wide meeting on SoTL research, and I applied for their faculty learning community during my first tenure-track year.

During my experience in the SoTL Learning Community, I used the processes described in this book with great success. With structure and guidance to keep me moving forward, I was able to construct my first SoTL pilot project. Because of the deadlines we were held to as a group, I completed the first year of my study and presented my project at a peer-reviewed conference right away. Although this may not sound very impressive to some readers, I can assure you it meant a great deal to me. By realizing that I could do SoTL work and that research was *not* beyond my scope, it allowed me to believe that I could do more. And so I did! I was able to present at two more teaching-learning conferences and at two sessions presented to faculty at my university. Again, by having a few small successes, my confidence in and passion for teaching and learning began to grow. I suddenly became able to identify myself as an educator (versus a nurse), and I began to feel that I "fit" into the culture that is academia.

In the spring of 2010, just as our semester was coming to a close, I met with a potential community partner for the fall. As a result of my two years as a SoTL researcher, I knew that service learning could be done in a better way than I had been doing it. I had a great basis for student involvement (and evaluation), but I was "re-creating the wheel" each and every semester, as I set up clinical rotations with new community agencies. I could not get a firm commitment about my students until weeks before the semester started and had to constantly revise our schedule as dates and times fell through, or as my students were forgotten about or overlooked due to agency issues. This time, because I had taken the time to reflect on my experiences, I knew what I needed in a partner.

During the first 20 minutes of our meeting, the executive director of our local YWCA committed to a partnership and passed along some information about a grant. As I looked at the application materials, I realized that my background as a nurse-midwife would be a natural fit for a project that would cover teen pregnancy and STD prevention. I also knew, from my two previous SoTL studies, that with my guidance, my junior-level nursing students could implement the program and could benefit through the reciprocal nature of service learning. The YWCA director and I spent the next month working together and exploring our partnership as we wrote the grant. At a very early point in our relationship, we had to have difficult conversations about roles, expectations, and budgets. We were shocked (and excited) to learn that we received the grant, for over $2 million, for this five-year project. I never imagined the work I'd done to develop my understanding and interest in service learning, through my very first SoTL project, would lead to this amazing opportunity! Without my well-defined, well-refined project, I could never have visualized the details of this program, and I never would have had the confidence to try.

I wholeheartedly believe in the organization and the effectiveness of the tools in this book. Without the structure and support provided, I'm afraid I'd still be doing literature reviews and trying to decide on an area of interest! Beyond my great experience with SoTL research and the validation of the impact it has on my teaching, I have found a way to tie my teaching, scholarship, and service together into one cohesive package. I can hardly talk about one area without talking about the other two! Through this service-learning project, I will be studying outcomes for the clients we serve (from a disciplinary standpoint) and the outcomes for my students (through the SoTL piece), and

everything I do will inform and have an impact on my scholarship. The amazing thing is that the SoTL project I originally developed during my faculty learning community is the *same* one I'm using today! When I first began discussing SoTL with Drs. Dietz-Uhler and Bishop-Clark, I remember their introducing the concept of "phasing" one's work. This is exactly what I've been able to replicate; I don't have to create project after project after project. I worked really hard at developing an idea that can be applied in about a million different ways, and I keep tweaking it, adding to it, and exploring it a little differently. This makes it possible to keep something going all the time, and it certainly cuts down on my time when it comes to IRB applications and conference proposals.

One final outcome from my SoTL work that I have to mention is that it has led to my development of a new "Partnership Model," a framework that encourages faculty members to become authentic partners with their associated community agency. It allows the synergy created by the university and that agency to do bigger and better things that reach beyond that agency's service population. More interesting, though, is that it moves the *student* to the position of partner. I have made it my mission to involve students in every aspect of my work. During the pilot year of my project, I have students functioning as undergraduate associates, pilot presenters, and undergraduate research assistants. These students are actively involved in every single thing I do, which I believe is a priceless experience during a busy undergraduate program. They are assisting with revision of curriculum for the program, IRB revision work, writing small grants, implementing the program, writing proposals and abstracts for professional conferences, and presenting at these conferences. I have made it a priority to teach my students about my own processes, even if I don't consider myself to be the authority. I am willing to look a little foolish at times, to learn alongside them, and to let students *in* as I figure things out. This means they get an opportunity, through experiential learning, to pull themselves along as leaders. They are valued, they are respected, and they are stepping up to exceed my expectations at every turn. The leadership skills they are developing are incredible. They will be more confident and more experienced critical thinkers as they interview for their first positions next year, and as they become educators themselves, in one capacity or another.

Appendix A: SoTL Conferences

Conferences list compiled from the following:

Florida State College (www.teachlearn.org/), Illinois State (www.sotl.ilstu.edu/sotlConf/) and University of Central Florida (www.fctl.ucf.edu/ResearchAndScholarship/Conferences/)

- 3rd Annual Conference on Higher Education Pedagogy:
  http://www.cider.vt.edu/conference/
- 4th Annual SoTL Commons Conference:
  http://academics.georgiasouthern.edu/ijsotl/conferencc/2011/
- 22nd International Conference on College Teaching and Learning:
  http://www.teachlearn.org/
- American Council on Education:
  http://www.aceannualmeeting.org/
- American Educational Research Association (AERA):
  http://www.aera.net/meetings/Default.aspx?menu_id=22&id=50
- Annual Conference on Distance Teaching and Learning:
  http://www.uwex.edu/disted/conference/
- Annual Conference on The First-Year Experience:
  http://www.sc.edu/fye/
- Association for the Advancement of Sustainability in Higher Education (AASHE):
  http://conf2010.aashe.org/aashe2011-notifications
- Association of American Colleges and Universities (AAC&U):
  http://www.aacu.org/meetings/index.cfm
- EduCause Annual Conference:
  http://net.educause.edu/node/31
- Frontiers in Education (FIE):
  http://fie-conference.org/fie2011/
- International Conference on Academic Integrity:
  http://www.academicintegrity.org/index.php
- International Society for the Scholarship of Teaching and Learning Annual Conference:
  http://issotl10.indiana.edu/index.html
- International Studies Association's Annual Convention:
  http://www.isanet.org/
- Instructional Technology Council: eLearning Annual Conference:
  http://www.itcnetwork.org/elearning-conference.html
- Lilly Conference on College and University Teaching (North):
  http://facit.cmich.edu/
- Lilly West 2011 Conference:
  http://www.iats.com/conferences/west/index.shtml
- National Education Association Annual Meeting:
  http://www.nea.org/annualmeeting/index.html
- Professional and Organizational Development Network in Higher Education (POD):
  http://www.podnetwork.org/conferences.htm
- Southern Regional Faculty and Instructional Development Consortium (SRFIDC):
  http://www.srfidc.org/index.php
- The Chair Academy's Annual International Conference:
  http://www.chairacademy.com/index.html
- The Collaboration for Learning Annual Conference:
  http://www.thecollaborationforlearning.org/home
- The SoTL Commons: A Conference for the Scholarship of Teaching and Learning:
  http://academics.georgiasouthern.edu/ijsotl/conference/ 2011/index.htm
- The Sun Conference on Learning and Teaching:
  http://cetalweb.utep.edu/sun/
- The Teaching Professor Annual Conference:
  http://www.teachingprofessor.com/conference
- The Twelfth Annual Midwest Conference on the Scholarship of Teaching and Learning:
  http://www.iusb.edu/~ucet/sotl.shtml

Appendix B: SoTL Journals

Core SoTL journals compiled from the following:

Buffalo State-SUNY
(http://buffalostate.edu/orgs/castl/publish.html),
Illinois State University-Milner Library (http://ilstu
.libguides.com/sotl), McKinney (2007)

Academic Commons (website)
Academic Exchange Quarterly
Active Learning in Higher Education
American Educational Research Journal
American Journal of Distance Education
American Journal of Education
Arts and Humanities in Higher Education
ASHE-ERIC Higher Education Report
Assessment Update
Black Issues in Higher Education
Canadian Journal for the Scholarship of Teaching and
  Learning
Change: The Magazine of Higher Learning
Chronicle of Higher Education
College Student Journal
College Teaching
Comparative Education
Currents in Teaching and Learning (online journal)
Deliberations (website)
Educational Forum
Educational Researcher
Effective Teaching: The Carolina Colloquy's Electronic
  Journal of University Teaching and Learning
Feminist Teacher
F-LIGHT (E-newsletter from the TLT Group)
Harvard Educational Review
Higher Education Perspectives
Higher Education Research and Development
Innovate
Innovation in Education and Training International
Innovative Higher Education
InSight (online journal)

Interdisciplinary Journal of Problem-based Learning
  (IFPBL) (online journal)
International Journal for Academic Development
International Journal for the Scholarship of Teaching and
  Learning (online journal)
International Journal of Teaching and Learning in Higher
  Education (online journal)
International Journal on Teaching and Learning in Higher
  Education
Inventio: Creative Thinking About Teaching and Learning
  (online journal)
Journal for the Art of Teaching
Journal of Blacks in Higher Education
Journal of Cognitive and Affective Learning (JCAL)
  (online journal)
Journal of College and Character
Journal of College Student Development
Journal of Effective Teaching (online journal)
Journal of Faculty Development
Journal of General Education
Journal of Graduate Teaching Assistant Development
Journal of Higher Education
Journal of Negro Education
Journal of Public Service and Outreach
Journal of Scholarship of Teaching and Learning
  (online journal)
Journal of Student-Centered Learning
Journal of Teaching and Learning
Journal of the First-Year Experience and Students in
  Transition
Journal of University Teaching and Learning Practice
  (JUTLP) (online journal)
Journal on Excellence in College Teaching
LATISS—Learning and Teaching in the Social Sciences
Learning and Instruction
Learning and Teaching in Higher Education (LATHE)
  (online journal)
Learning Inquiry
Liberal Education

Michigan Journal of Community Service Learning
MountainRise (online journal)
National Teaching and Learning Forum (NTLF)
New Chalk
New Directions for Teaching and Learning
OTH on-line (online journal)
Perspectives on Undergraduate Research and Mentoring (PURM) (online journal)
Planning for Higher Education
Practice and Evidence of the Scholarship of Teaching and Learning in Higher Education (online journal)
Reaching Through Teaching (online journal)
Research in Higher Education
Review of Educational Research

Review of Higher Education
Studies in Graduate and Professional Student Development (formerly *Journal of Graduate Teaching Assistant Development*)
Studies in Higher Education
Teaching Ethics
Teaching Excellence
Teaching in Higher Education
Teaching Professor
The Successful Professor
To Improve the Academy
Transformative Dialogues: Teaching and Learning Journal (online journal)
VCU Teaching (online journal)

Appendix C: Disciplinary Journals

Disciplinary journals compiled from the following:

Abilene Christian University (http://acu.edu/academics/ library/sotl.html), Center for Faculty Evaluation & Development Division of Continuing Education Kansas State University (www.theideacenter.org/ sites/default/files/Idea_Paper_28.pdf), Indiana University Bloomington Libraries (http://libraries .iub.edu/index.php?pageId=1002175), McKinney (2007)

Accounting
Issues in Accounting Education
Journal of Accounting Education

African American Studies
Black Scholar: Journal of Black Studies and Research
International Journal of Africana Studies
Journal of Black Studies
Western Journal of Black Studies

Agricultural Engineering/ Agricultural Mechanization
Applied Engineering in Agriculture
The Journal of Agricultural Mechanization

Agriculture
Journal of Agricultural Education (online journal)
Journal of Agricultural Education and Extension
NACTA Journal

Agronomy
Journal of Natural Resources and Life Sciences Education
NACTA Journal

Anthropology
Anthropology and Education Quarterly

Architecture
International Journal of Technology and Design Education
Journal of Architectural Education
TIES

Art Education
Art Education
Arts Education Policy Review
Dance Teacher
European Journal of Arts Education
International Journal of Art and Design Education
Journal of Aesthetic Education
Journal of Aesthetics and Art Criticism
Journal of Social Theory in Art Education
Studies of Art Education

Behavioral Science
Behavioral Science Teacher
Journal of Applied Behavioral Science
Small Group Behavior
Small Group Research

Biochemistry
Biochemical Education
Biochemistry and Molecular Biology Education

Biology
Advances in Physiology Education
American Biology Teacher
Bioscience
Cell Biology Education
Journal of Biological Education

Business and Economics
Accounting Education
Business Education Forum
Delta Pi Epsilon Journal
Focus on Business Education

International Journal of Accounting Education and Research
International Review for Business Education
Issues in Accounting Education
Journal of Accounting Education
Journal of Applied Research for Business Instruction
Journal of Business Education
Journal of Economic Education
Journal of Education for Business
Journal of Language for International Business
Journal of Management Education
Journal of Marketing Education
Journal of Teaching in International Business
Marketing Education Review
NABTE Review (National Association of Business Teacher Education)
Organizational Behavior Teaching Review
Social Education/The Journal of National Council for the Social Studies
Statistics Education Research Journal
Teaching Business Ethics
Teaching Economist

Chemistry

Chemical Educator
Chemical Engineering Education
Education in Chemistry
Journal of Chemical Education

Chiropractic

Journal of Chiropractic Education

College Student Personnel

Journal of College Student Development
NASPA Journal (National Association of Student Personnel Administrators)

Communications/Speech

Canadian Journal of Educational Communication
Communication Education
Communication Teacher
Innovations in Teaching and Learning Information and Computer Sciences
Journalism and Mass Communication Educator
Media and Methods

Computer Science

Active Learning
Computer Science Education
Computers and Education
Journal of Computer Science Education

Journal of Computers in Mathematics and Science Teaching
Journal of Information Systems Education
Mathematics and Computer Education

Construction Science

ASHRAE Journal (American Society of Heating, Refrigeration, and Air Conditioning Engineers)
ENR: Engineering News Record
IES LDA (Illuminating Engineering Society—Lighting Design plus Application)

Counseling

Counseling Psychology
Counselor Education and Supervision
Journal of Counseling and Development

Criminal Justice

Journal of Criminal Justice Education

Dentistry

Bulletin of Dental Education
Journal of Dental Education

Design & Graphics/Interior Architecture/Interior Design

Journal of Interior Design
Journal of Interior Design Education and Research
Representation

Dietetics

Journal of Nutrition Education
Journal of the American Dietetic Association

Drama

Research in Drama Education
Theatre Topics

Education

Action in Teacher Education
Advances in Teacher Education
American Educational Research Journal
Assessment and Evaluation in Higher Education
Better Teaching
Black Issues in Higher Education
British Journal of Sociology of Education
California Educator
Canadian Journal of Higher Education
Classroom Connect
Classroom Leadership
Community College Journal of Research and Practice

Core Teacher
Critical Issues in Teacher Education
Curriculum Journal
Curriculum Studies
Educating for Employment
Educational Action Research
Educational Pathways
Effective School Practices
Focus on Education
General Educator
IEEE Transactions on Education (Institute of Electrical and Electronics Engineering)
Independent Scholar
Insights into Open Education
Instructional Science
Instructional Strategies: An Applied Research Series
International Journal of Curriculum and Instruction
Internet and Higher Education
JCT
Journal of Blacks in Higher Education
Journal of Curriculum and Supervision
Journal of Curriculum Studies
Journal of Education for Teaching
Journal of Engineering Education
Journal of Experimental Education
Journal of Higher Education
Journal of Information Technology for Teacher Education
Journal of Interactive Instruction Development
Journal of Interactive Learning Research
Journal of Interdisciplinary Studies
Journal of Negro Education
Journal of Teacher Education
Journal of the Scholarship of Teaching and Learning
Journal of Visual Literacy
Liberal Education
Mentoring and Tutoring
MountainRise
On the Horizon
Open Learning
Papers and Recordings in Education
Paths of Learning
Peace Education
Professional Development Collection
Quarterly Review of Distance Education
Radical Pedagogy
Research in Developmental Education
Review of Educational Research
Studies in Higher Education
Syllabus
Teacher Development
Teacher Education and Practice
Teacher Education and Special Education

Teacher Education Quarterly
Teacher Educator
Teachers and Teaching: Theory and Practice
Teaching and Change
Teaching and Learning: The Journal of Natural Inquiry
Teaching and Teacher Education
Teaching College
THE Journal: Technological Horizons in Education
Transformations: The Journal of Inclusive Scholarship and Pedagogy
What Works in Teaching and Learning

Engineering & Technology

ASEE Prism (American Society for Engineering Education)
ASHRAE Journal (American Society for Heating, Refrigeration, Air Conditioning Engineers)
Chemical Engineering Education
Curriculum • Technology Quarterly
Engineering Education
Engineering Education and Research
ENR: Engineering News Record
From Now On—the Educational Technology Journal
IEEE Transactions on Education (Institute of Electrical and Electronics Engineering)
IES LDA (Illuminating Engineering Society—Lighting Design plus Application)
Innovations in Science Education and Technology
International Journal of Electrical Engineering Education
International Journal of Instructional Media
Journal of Chemical Engineering
Journal of Design and Technology Education
Journal of Educational Multimedia and Hypermedia
Journal of Engineering Education
Journal of Technology Education
Learning and Leading with Technology
Literacy
Simile—Studies in Media & Information Literacy
Technical Communication Quarterly
Technology Teacher

English

ADE (Association of Departments of English) *Bulletin*
Assessing Writing
College Composition and Communication
College English
Composition Studies
ELT Journal
English Education
English in Education
English Leadership Quarterly

English Quarterly
English Teaching Forum
Journal of English for Academic Purposes
Journal of Intensive English Studies
Journal of Teaching Writing
Modern English Teacher
North Carolina English Teacher
Ohio Reading Teacher
Pedagogy
Reading Research and Instruction
Research in the Teaching of English
Teaching English in the Two-Year College
Trends and Issues in Postsecondary English Studies

English as a Second Language

Annual Editions: Teaching English as a Second Language
College ESL
Hispania
TESOL Journal (Teachers of English to Speakers of Other Languages)
TESOL Quarterly (Teachers of English to Speakers of Other Languages)

Environmental Studies

Environmental Education and Information
International Research in Geographical and Environmental Education
Journal of Environmental Education

Family Studies & Consumer Science

Family and Consumer Sciences Educator
Family Relations
Journal of Extension
Journal of Family and Consumer Sciences Education
Journal of Teaching in Marriage and Family

Finance

Financial Practice & Education
Journal of Financial Education

Foods/Nutrition

Journal of Nutrition Education (not directed to higher education)

Geography & Geology

Journal of Geography
Journal of Geography in Higher Education
Journal of Geological Education
Journal of Geoscience Education
Teaching Geography

Gerontology

Educational Gerontology
Gerontology and Geriatrics Education

Health, Kinesiology, Physical Education

Advances in Health Education: Current Research
Advances in Health Sciences Education
Advances in Physiology Education
American Journal of Health Education
European Journal of Physical Education
European Physical Education Review
Health Educator
Journal of Food Science Education
Journal of Health Administration Education
Journal of Health Education
Journal of Nutrition Education
Journal of Nutrition Education and Behavior
Journal of Physical Education, Recreation & Dance
Journal of Teaching in Physical Education
Journal of Teaching Physical Education Strategies
Physical Educator
Quest

History

History Teacher
International Review of History Education
Journal of American History
Teaching History
Teaching History: A Journal of Methods
Teaching of History

Instructional Design

Syllabus
THE Journal: Technological Horizons in Education

Journalism

Journalism and Mass Communication Educator
Journalism Educator
Media and Methods

Law

CLE (Continuing Legal Education) *Journal*
Journal of Legal Education
Learning and the Law

Library & Information Science

Journal of Education for Librarianship
Journal of Education for Library and Information Science
Research Strategies
Simile—Studies in Media & Information Literacy
Teaching Librarian

Mathematics & Statistics

AMATYC Review
American Statistician
Arithmetic Teacher
College Mathematics Journal
Educational Studies in Mathematics
Journal for Research in Mathematics Education
Journal of Mathematics Teacher Education
Journal of Statistics Education
Mathematics and Computer Education
Mathematics Educator
Mathematics Teacher
Mathematics Teaching
Mathematics Teaching in the Middle School
PRIMUS (Problems, Resources and Issues in
    Undergraduate Mathematics Study)
Research in Collegiate Mathematics Education
School Science and Mathematics
SSMA Topics for Teachers Monograph Series
Statistics Education Research Journal
STATS
Teaching Children Mathematics
Teaching Mathematics and Its Applications
Teaching Statistics
The American Statistician
TME (The Mathematics Educator)

Medicine

Academic Medicine
Advances in Physiology Education
American Journal of Pharmaceutical Education
Journal of Pharmacy Teaching
Medical Education
Medical Education Online
Medical Teacher
New Learning Medicine
Pharmacy Student
Teaching and Learning in Medicine

Modern Languages & Linguistics

ACTFL Foreign Language Education Series
ADFL Bulletin (Association of Departments of Foreign
    Languages)
Association of Teachers of Japanese
Canadian Modern Language Review
Computer-Assisted Language Learning
Foreign Language Annals
French Review
International Review of Applied Linguistics
IRAL: International Review of Applied Linguistics
Journal of French Language Studies
Language and Education

Language and Learning for Human Service Professions
Language Teaching
Language Teaching Research
Lingua Franca
Modern Language Journal
Studies in Modern Languages Education
The IALLT Journal of Language Learning Technologies

Music

British Journal of Music Education
Contributions to Music Education
Council for Research in Music Education
Current Issues in Music Education
Illinois Music Educator
Indiana Musicator
Instrumentalist
International Journal of Music Education
Journal of Music Theory Pedagogy
Journal of Research in Music Education
Journal of Singing
Mississippi Music Educator
Missouri Journal of Research in Music Education
Music Education Research
Music Educators Journal
Music Teacher
Philosophy of Music Education Review
Piano Journal
Teaching Music
Update: Applications of Research in Music Education

Nursing

Image: Journal of Nursing Scholarships
Journal of Continuing Education in Nursing
Journal of Nursing Education
Nurse Education in Practice
Nurse Educator
Nursing and Health Science Education Review
Review of Research in Nursing Education

Pharmacy

American Journal of Pharmaceutical Education
Pharmacy Education

Philosophy

Metaphilosophy
Teaching Philosophy

Physics

American Journal of Physics
Physics Education
Physics Teacher

Physiology

Advances in Physiology Education

Political Science

Journal of Political Science Education
PS: Political Science and Politics (incorporated Political
   Science Teacher)

Psychology & Psychiatry

Academic Psychiatry (formerly the *Journal of Psychiatric*
   Education)
American Psychiatry
Behavioral Educator
Behavioral Science Teacher
British Journal of Educational Studies
Cognition and Instruction
Counseling Psychology
Counselor Education and Supervision
Educational Psychologist
Journal of Applied Behavioral Science
Journal of Educational Psychology
Journal of Instructional Psychology
Small Group Research
Teaching of Psychology

Public Administration/Regional
& Community Planning

Journal of Planning Education and Research
Journal of the American Planning Association
Teaching Public Administration

Recreation & Tourism

Chef Educator Today
Hospitality & Tourism Educator
Journal of Hospitality, Leisure, Sport and Tourism
   Education
Journal of Teaching in Travel and Tourism
Schole: A Journal of Leisure Studies & Recreation
   Education

Religion/Theology

Christian Educators Journal
Christian School Education
Dialogue on Campus
Journal of Moral Education
Religion Teachers Journal
Religious Education
Teaching Theology and Religion
Theological Education

Sciences

Instructional Science: An International Journal of
   Learning and Cognition
International Journal of Science Education
Journal of College Science Teaching
Journal of Environmental Education
Journal of Research in Science Teaching
Journal of Science Education and Technology
Oregon Science Teacher
Research in Science and Technological Education
School Science and Mathematics
Science Education
Science Teacher
Science Teacher Education
Studies in Science Education

Social Studies

Social Education/The Journal of National Council for the
   Social Studies
Theory and Research in Social Education

Social Work

Compendium of Resources for Teaching About the
   Nonprofit Sector, Voluntarism and Philanthropy
Issues in Social Work Education
Journal of Education for Social Work
Journal of Social Work Education
Journal of Teaching in Social Work
Social Work Education Reporter

Sociology

International Studies in Sociology of Education
Learning and Teaching in the Social Sciences
Sociology of Education
Teaching and Learning Matters
Teaching Sociology

Theater

Theatre Topics
Youth Theatre Journal

Veterinary Medicine

Journal of Medical Education
Journal of the American Veterinary Medical Association
Journal of Veterinary Medical Education

Women's Studies

Feminist Teacher

Appendix D: Journals About Higher Education in General

Journals about higher education in general compiled from the following:

Abilene Christian University (http://acu.edu/academics/ library/sotl.html); Center for Faculty Evaluation & Development Division of Continuing Education, Kansas State University (www.theideacenter.org/sites/default/ files/Idea_Paper_ 28.pdf)

AAHE Bulletin (American Association for Higher Education)
Academe
Adult Education
Adult Education Quarterly
Adult Leadership
Adult Learning
Assessment and Evaluation in Higher Education
Carson—Newman Studies
College and University
College Freshman
College Quarterly
College Research
Community and Junior College Journal
Community College Journal
Community College Journal of Research and Practice
Community-Junior College Research Quarterly
Computers in Human Behavior
Continuing Higher Education Review
Cooperative Learning and College Teaching Newsletter
Current Issues in Catholic Higher Education
Educational Leadership
Educational Record
Educational Studies
Educational Technology
Educational Technology Research and Development
Education Next
Higher Education
Higher Education Abstracts
Hispanic Outlook in Higher Education
History of Higher Education Annual
Initiatives

Journal of Adult Education
Journal of Applied Research in the Community College
Journal of Blacks in Higher Education
Journal of Classroom Interaction
Journal of College Literacy and Learning
Journal of Creative Behavior
Journal of Developmental Education
Journal of Educational Research
Journal of Education and Christian Belief
Journal of Education for Students Placed at Risk
Journal of Excellence in College Teaching
Journal of Excellence in Higher Education
Journal of Further and Higher Education
Journal of Instructional Development
Journal of Staff, Program, and Organizational Development
Journal of the National Academic Advising Association
Journal of Vocational and Technical Education
The Kappan—Phi Delta Kappan
Leadership Educational
Liberal Education
NASPA Journal (National Association of Student Personnel Administrators)
National Teaching & Learning Forum
NCA Quarterly
New Academic
New Directions for Community Colleges
New Directions for Higher Education
Personnel and Guidance Journal
Quality in Higher Education
Resources in Education (ERIC Clearinghouse abstracts)
Review of Research in Education
Simulation & Games
Simulation/Gaming/News
Society for Values in Higher Education (Monograph Series)
Studies in Continuing Education
Teachers College Record
Technology & Learning
Telescan
Tertiary Education and Management
Training and Development Journal
Women in Higher Education

References

American Psychological Association. (1982). *Ethical principles in the conduct of research with human participants.* Washington, DC: Author.

Association of American Colleges & Universities (AAC&U). (2008). Our *students' best work: A framework for accountability worthy of our mission* (2nd ed.). Washington, DC: Author.

Bass, R. (1999). The scholarship of teaching: What's the problem? *Creative Thinking about Learning and Teaching, 1*(1), 1–10.

Baxter Magolda, M. B. (1999). *Creating contexts for learning and self-authorship: Constructive development pedagogy.* Nashville, TN: Vanderbilt University Press.

Baxter Magolda, M. B. (2001). *Making their own way: Narratives for transforming higher education to promote self-development.* Sterling, VA: Stylus.

Bennett, J. O., Briggs, W. L., & Triola, M. F. (2009). *Statistical reasoning for everyday life.* Boston, MA: Pearson Addison Wesley.

Berg, B. L. (2007). *Qualitative research methods for the social sciences* (6th ed.). Boston, MA: Pearson.

Bernstein, D. (2010). Finding your place in the scholarship of teaching and learning. *International Journal for the Scholarship of Teaching and Learning, 4*(2), 1–6.

Bishop-Clark, C. (1992). Protocol analysis of a novice programmer. *SIGSCE Bulletin, 24*(3), 14–18.

Bishop-Clark, C. (1995). Cognitive style and its effect on the stages of computer programming. *Journal of Research on Computing in Education, 27*(4), 373–386.

Bishop-Clark, C. (1998). Comparing understanding of programming design concepts using visual basic and traditional basic. *Journal of Educational Computing Research, 18*(1), 37–47.

Bishop-Clark, C. (2006). Problem-based service learning in a 200-level systems analysis and design course. *Information Systems Education Journal, 4*(100).

Bishop-Clark, C., Courte, J., & Howard, E. (2006). Programming in pairs with Alice to improve confidence, enjoyment and achievement. *Journal of Educational Computing Research, 34*(2), 213–228.

Bishop-Clark, C., Courte, J., Evans, D., & Howard, E. (2007). A quantitative and qualitative investigation of using Alice programming to improve confidence, enjoyment and achievement among non-majors. *Journal of Educational Computing Research, 37*(2), 193–207.

Bishop-Clark, C., & Dietz-Uhler, B. (2003). Forming online impressions: A class exercise. *Journal of Educational Technology Systems, 31*(3), 251–260.

Bishop-Clark, C., & Wheeler, D. (1994). The Myers Briggs Personality Type and its relationship to computer programming. *Journal of Research on Computer in Education, 26*(3), 358–37.

Black, C. (2010). *The dynamic classroom: Engaging students in higher education.* Madison, WI: Atwood.

Bordens, K. S., & Abbott, B. B. (2008). *Research methods and design: A process approach* (7th ed.). Boston, MA: McGraw-Hill.

Boud, D., Keogh, R., & Walker, D. (1985). *Reflection: Turning experience into learning.* London, UK: Kogan Page.

Boyer, E. L. (1990). *Scholarship reconsidered: Priorities of the professoriate.* San Francisco, CA: Jossey-Bass.

Bransford, J., National Research Council (U.S.), & National Research Council (U.S.). (2000). *How people learn: Brain, mind, experience, and school.* Washington, DC: National Academy Press.

Braxton, J. M., Luckey, W., & Helland, P. (2002). Institutionalizing a broader view of scholarship through Boyer's four domains. *ASHE-ERIC Higher Education Report, 29*(2). San Francisco, CA: Jossey-Bass.

Brookfield, S. D. (2005). *Becoming a critically reflective thinker.* San Francisco, CA: Jossey-Bass.

Campbell, D., & Stanley, J. (1963). *Experimental and quasi-experimental designs for research.* Boston, MA: Houghton Mifflin Company.

Chism, N. V. N. (2008, April). The scholarship of teaching and learning: Implications for professional development. Key presentation at the Thai Professional and Organizational Development (POD) Network 2-Day Workshop, Bangkok, Thailand.

Chism, N., & Sanders, D. (1986). The place of practice-centered inquiry in faculty development. In M. Svinicki (Ed.), *To improve the academy, Vol. 6* (pp. 56–64). Stillwater, OK: New Forums.

Chizmar, J. (2005). The effectiveness of assignments that utilize a time-efficient grading scheme. *Journal on Excellence in College Teaching, 16,* 5–21.

Clark, R. A., & Jones, D. (2001). A comparison of traditional and on-line formats in a public speaking course. *Communication Education, 50*(2), 109–124.

Clinton, B. D., & Kohlmeyer, M. (2005). The effects of group quizzes on performance and motivation to learn: Two experiments in cooperative learning. *Journal of Accounting Education, 23*(2), 96–116.

Considine, J. R., Meyers, R. A., & Timerman, C. E. (2006). Evidence use in group quiz discussions: How do students support preferred choices? *Journal on Excellence in College Teaching, 17*(3), 65–89.

Cook, T., & Campbell, D. (1979). *Quasi-experimentation: Design and analysis issues for field settings.* Boston, MA: Wadsworth.

Cooper, S., Dann, W., & Pausch, R. (2003). Teaching objects-first in introductory computer science. *Proceedings of the 34th SIGCSE technical symposium on computer science education,* Reno, NV.

Creswell, J. W., & Plano Clark, V. L. (2007). Designing and conducting mixed methods research. Thousand Oaks, CA: Sage.

Cross, K. P. (1986, September). A proposal to improve teaching: Or, what taking "teaching seriously" should mean. *AAHE Bulletin, 39*(1), 9–14.

Crouch, C. H., & Mazur, E. (2001). Peer instruction: Ten years of experience and results. *American Journal of Physics, 69,* 970–977.

Crutcher, R. J. (1994). Telling what we know: The use of verbal report methodologies in psychological research. *Psychological Science, 5*(5), 241–244.

Davies, M. B. (2007). Doing *a successful research project: Using qualitative or quantitative methods.* New York: Palgrave Macmillan.

Denton, B., Adams, C., Blatt, P., & Lorish, C. (2000). Does the introduction of problem-based learning change graduate performance outcomes in a professional curriculum? *Journal on Excellence in College Teaching, 11*(2&3), 147–162.

Dewey, J. (1933). *How we think.* New York: Prometheus.

Diamond, R. M. (1993). Changing priorities and the faculty reward system. In R. M. Diamond and B. E. Adam (Eds.), *Recognizing faculty work: Reward systems for the year 2000* (pp. 5–23). New Directions for Higher Education, No. 81. San Francisco: Jossey-Bass.

Dietz-Uhler, B. (2008). Effectiveness of a web-based critical thinking module. In D. S. Dunn, J. S. Halonen, & R. A. Smith (Eds.), *Teaching critical thinking in psychology: A handbook of best practices* (pp. 273–276). West Sussex, UK: Wiley-Blackwell.

Dietz-Uhler, B., & Bishop-Clark, C. (2001). The use of computer-mediated communication to enhance subsequent face-to-face discussions. *Computers in Human Behavior, 17*(3), 269–283.

Dietz-Uhler, B., & Bishop-Clark, C. (2002). The psychology of computer-mediated communication: Four classroom exercises. *Psychology Learning and Teaching, 2,* 25–31.

Dietz-Uhler, B., Bishop-Clark, C., & Fisher, A. (2002). The effects of online versus face-to-face course delivery on performance and satisfaction. Unpublished manuscript. Miami University, Oxford, OH.

Dietz-Uhler, B., Bishop-Clark, C., & Howard, E. (2005). Formation of and adherence to a self-disclosure norm in an online chat. *CyberPsychology and Behavior, 8,* 114–120.

Dietz-Uhler, B., & Lanter, R. (2009). Using the four-questions technique to enhance learning. *Teaching of Psychology, 36,* 38–41.

Doyle, T. (2008). *Helping students learn in a learner-centered environment: A guide to facilitating learning in higher education.* Sterling, VA: Stylus.

Edmonds, O. P. (1982). The heart rate of students in examinations. *Occupational Medicine, 32,* 32–36.

Elton, L. (2008). Recognition and acceptance of the scholarship of teaching and learning. *International Journal for the Scholarship of Teaching and Learning, 2*(1), 1–5.

Evans, R. C., & Omaha Boy, N. H. (1996). Abandoning the lecture in biology. *Journal on Excellence in College Teaching, 7*(3), 93–110.

Finlay, S., & Faulkner, G. (2005). Tête à tête: Reading groups and peer learning. *Active Learning in Higher Education, 6*(1), 32–45.

Fleming, V. M. (2001). Helping students learn to learn by using a check list, modified rubrics, and e-mail. *Journal on Excellence in College Teaching, 12*(1), 5–22.

Fowler, F. J. (2009). *Survey research methods.* Thousand Oaks, CA: Sage.

Frechtling, J., & Westat, L. S. (1997). *User-friendly handbook for mixed methods research.* Retrieved May 19, 2010, from http://www.nsf.gov/pubs/1997/nsf97153/start.htm

Gallos, J. V. (2008). Charting a new course for the scholarship of teaching and learning: Future directions, powerful opportunities, a hopeful future. *Journal of Management Education, 32*(5), 535–540.

Gelmon, S., & Agre-Kippenhan, S. (2002). Promotion, tenure, and the engaged scholar. *AAHE Bulletin,*

7–11. Retrieved December 2, 2010, from http://www.artsci.utk.edu/outreach/pdfs

Gilpin, L., & Liston, D. (2009). Transformative education in the scholarship of teaching and learning: An analysis of the SoTL literature. *International Journal for the Scholarship of Teaching and Learning, 3*(2), 1–8.

Glaser, B. G., & Strauss, A. L. (1967). *The discovery of grounded theory: Strategies for qualitative research.* New York: Aldine.

Glassick, C. E., Huber, M. T., & Maeroff, G. I. (1997). *Scholarship assessed: Evaluation of the professoriate.* San Francisco, CA: Jossey-Bass.

Gordon, G. (2010). SoTL and the quality agenda. *International Journal for the Scholarship of Teaching and Learning, 4*(2), 1–6.

Grauerholz, L., & Zipp, J. F. (2008). How to do the scholarship of teaching and learning. *Teaching Sociology, 36,* 87–94.

Gurm, B. K. (2009). Is all scholarship equally valued? Fusion of horizons on the definition and status of scholarship. *International Journal for the Scholarship of Teaching and Learning, 3*(2), 1–10.

Gurung, R. A. R., & Schwartz, B. M. (2010). Riding the third wave of SoTL. *International Journal for the Scholarship of Teaching and Learning, 4*(2), 1–6.

Hart, F. R. (1990). *Beyond the books: Reflections on learning and teaching.* Columbus, OH: Ohio State University Press.

Hake, R. R. 1998a. Interactive-engagement vs traditional methods: A six-thousand-student survey of mechanics test data for introductory physics courses. *American Journal of Physics* 66:64-74. Retrieved from http://www.physics.indiana.edu/~sdi/ajpv3i.pdf

Hake, R. R. 1998b. *Interactive-engagement methods in introductory mechanics courses.* Retrieved from http://www.physics.indiana.edu/~sdi/IEM-2b.pdf

Healey, M. (2003). The scholarship of teaching: Issues around an evolving concept. *Journal on Excellence in College Teaching, 14*(2/3), 5–26.

Hestenes, D., & Wells, M. (1992). A mechanics baseline test. *Physics Teacher, 30*(3), 159–166.

Hestenes, D., Wells, M., & Swackhammer, G. (1992). Force concept inventory. *Physics Teacher, 30*(3), 141–151.

Huber, M. T. (2004). *Balancing acts: The scholarship of teaching and learning in academic careers.* Sterling, VA: Stylus.

Huber, M. T., & Hutchings, P. (2005). *The advancement of learning: Building the teaching commons.* San Francisco, CA: Jossey-Bass.

Hunt, S. K., Simonds, C. J., & Hinchliffe, L. J. (2000). Using student portfolios as authentic assessment of the basic communication course. *Journal on Excellence in College Teaching, 11*(1), 57–77.

Hutchings, P. (2000). *Opening lines: Approaches to the scholarship of teaching and learning.* Menlo Park, CA: Carnegie.

Hutchings, P. (2003). Competing goods: Ethical issues in the scholarship of teaching and learning. *Change,* September/October, 27–33.

Hutchings, P. (2010). Opening doors to faculty involvement in assessment (NILOA Occasional Paper No. 4). Urbana, IL: University of Illinois and Indiana University, National Institute of Learning Outcomes Assessment.

Hutchings, P., & Cambridge, B. (1999). *Your invitation to participate in the Carnegie Teaching Academy Campus Program.* Washington, DC: American Association for Higher Education and the Carnegie Foundation for the Advancement of Teaching.

Hutchings, P., & Huber, M. (2008). Placing theory in the scholarship of teaching and learning. *Arts and Humanities in Higher Education, 7,* 229–244.

Hutchings, P., Huber, M. T., & Ciccone, A. (2011). Getting there: An integrative vision of the scholarship of teaching and learning. *International Journal for the Scholarship of Teaching and Learning, 5*(1). Retrieved May 10, 2011, from http://www.georgiasouthern.edu/ijsotl

Hutchings, P., & Shulman, L. S. (1999). The scholarship of teaching and learning: New elaborations, new developments. *Change, 31*(5), 11–15.

Iaria, G., & Hubball, H. (2008). Assessing student engagement in small and large classes. *Transformative Dialogues Teaching & Learning Journal, 2*(1), 1–8.

Jackson, S. L. (2008). *Research methods: A modular approach.* Belmont, CA: Thomson Wadsworth.

Jay, J. K. (2003). *Quality teaching: Reflection at the heart of practice.* Lanham, MD: Scarecrow.

Jensen, E., & Jensen, E. (2008). *Brain-based learning: The new paradigm of teaching.* Thousand Oaks, CA: Corwin.

Kanuka, H. (2011). Keeping the scholarship in the scholarship of teaching and learning. *International Journal for the Scholarship of Teaching and Learning, 5*(1). Retrieved May 10, 2011, from http://www.georgiasouthern.edu/ijsotl

Kelleher, C., & Pausch, R. (2005). Lowering the barriers to programming: A taxonomy of programming environments and languages for novice programmers. *ACM Computing Surveys, 37*(2), 83–137.

Kelly-Kleese, C. (2003). Community college scholarship. *Journal on Excellence in College Teaching, 14*(2/3), 69–84.

Kiess, H. O., & Green, B. A. (2010). *Statistical concepts for the behavioral sciences.* Boston, MA: Allyn & Bacon.

Kreber, C. (2005). Charting a critical course on the scholarship of university teaching movement. *Studies in Higher Education, 30*(4), 389–405.

Kreber, C. (2006). Developing the scholarship of teaching through transformative learning. *Journal of the Scholarship of Teaching and Learning, 6*(1), 88–109.

Krueger, R. A., & Casey, M. A. (2000). *Focus groups: A practical guide for applied research.* Thousand Oaks, CA: Sage.

Kvale, S. (1996). *Interviews: An introduction to qualitative research interviewing.* Thousand Oaks, CA: Sage.

Light, R. J., Singer, J. D., & Willett, J. B. (1990). *By design: Planning research on higher education.* Cambridge, MA: Harvard University Press.

Lyman, F. (1981). The responsive classroom discussion. In A. S. Anderson (Ed.), *Mainstreaming digest.* College Park, MD: University of Maryland College of Education.

Lynch, J., & Bishop-Clark, C. (1993). Traditional and non-traditional student attitudes toward the mixed age college classroom. *Innovative Higher Education, 18*(2), 109–121.

Mack, N., Woodsong, C., MacQueen, K. M., Guest, G., & Namey, E. (2005). *Qualitative research methods: A data collectors' field guide.* Research Triangle Park, NC: Family Health International.

Marsh, P. A. (2007). What is known about student learning outcome and how does it relate to the scholarship of teaching and learning? *International Journal for the Scholarship of Teaching and Learning, 1*(2), 1–12.

Mason, A., Cohen, E., Yerushalmi, E., & Singh, C. (2008). Identifying differences in diagnostic skills between physics students: Developing a rubric. *Physical Education Research Conference, 1064,* 147–150.

Maurer, T. (2011). On publishing SoTL articles. *International Journal for the Scholarship of Teaching and Learning, 5*(1).

Mayring, P. (2000). Qualitative content analysis. *Forum: Qualitative Social Research, 1*(2), Art. 20. Retrieved from http://nbn-resolving.de/urn:nbn:de:0114-fqs 0002204

McConnell, C. M. (2004). Valuing the scholarship of teaching and learning in promotion and tenure reviews. In B. L. Cambridge (Ed.), *Campus progress: Supporting the scholarship of teaching and learning* (pp. 129–132). Washington, DC: American Association for Higher Education.

McDrury, J., & Alterio, M. (2003). *Learning through storytelling in higher education: Using reflection & experience to improve learning.* Sterling, VA: Taylor & Francis.

McKinney, K. (2002). The scholarship of teaching and learning: Current challenges and future visions. Retrieved December 15, 2010, from http://www.sotl .ilstu.edu/crossChair/sotlFuture.shtml

McKinney, K. (2007). *Enhancing learning through the scholarship of teaching and learning: The challenges and joys of juggling.* San Francisco, CA: Jossey-Bass/Anker.

McKinney, K. (2009). Lessons from my students and other reflections on SoTL. *International Journal for the Scholarship of Teaching and Learning, 3*(2), 1–3.

McKinney, K., and Jarvis, P. (2009). Beyond lines on the CV: Faculty applications of their scholarship of teaching and learning research. *International Journal of the Scholarship of Teaching and Learning, 3*(1), 1–13.

McLeod, S., Tulloch, M., Ritter, L., & Kent, J. (2005). Publishing scholarship in teaching & learning. *Proceedings of the Charles Stuart University learning & teaching conference.* Retrieved from http://www.csu .edu.au/faculty/educat/teached/staff/docs/McLeod etal(2005)CSUL&T.pdf

Medina, J. (2008). *Brain rules: 12 principles for surviving and thriving at work, home, and school.* Seattle, WA: Pear.

Millis, B. J., & Cottell, P.G. (1998). *Cooperative learning for higher education faculty.* American Council on Education/Oryx Press series on higher education. Phoenix, AZ: Oryx.

Moskel, B., Lurie, D., & Cooper, S. (2004). Evaluating the effectiveness of a new instructional approach. *Proceedings of the 35th SIGCSE technical symposium on computer science education* (pp. 75–79).

Nelson, C. (2003). Doing it: Examples of several of the different genres of the scholarship of teaching and learning. *Journal on Excellence in College Teaching, 14*(2 & 3), 85–94.

Newton, J. , Ginsburg, J., Rehner, J., Rogers, P., Sbrizzi, S., & Spencer, J. (Eds.) (2001). *Voices from the classroom: Reflections on teaching and learning in higher education.* Toronto, ON: Garamond Press.

Noppe, I., Achterberg, J., Duquaine, L., Huebbe, M., & Williams, C. (2007). PowerPoint presentation handouts and college student learning outcomes. *International Journal for the Scholarship of Teaching and Learning, 1*(1). Retrieved April 11, 2008, from http:// www.georgiasouthern.edu/ijsotl

O'Loughlin, V. D. (2002). Assessing the effects of using interactive learning activities in a large science class. *Journal of Excellence in College Teaching, 13*(1), 29–42.

Ovens, P., Wells, F., Wallis, P., & Hawkins, C. (2011). *Developing inquiry for learning: Reflection, collaboration and assessment in higher education.* New York: Routledge.

Pan, D. (2009). What scholarship of teaching? Why bother? *International Journal for the Scholarship of Teaching and Learning, 3*(1), 1–6.

Pate, M., & Miller, G. (2011). Effects of regulatory self-questioning on secondary-level students' problem-solving performance. *Journal of Agricultural Education, 52*(1), 72–84.

Patton, M. Q. (1987). *How to use qualitative methods in evaluation*. Newbury Park, CA: Sage.

Perry, W. G. (1970). *Forms of intellectual and ethical development in the college years: A scheme*. New York: Holt, Rinehart, and Winston.

Phillips, K. E. (2011). A performance enhanced interactive learning workshop model as a supplement for organic chemistry instruction. *Journal of College Science Teaching, 40*(3), 90–98.

Prehar, C. A., McCarthy, A. M., & Tucker, M. L. (2004). Predicting and changing student willingness to engage in community service. *Journal on Excellence in College Teaching, 15*(3), 63–83.

Randall, L. E., Buschner, C., & Swerkes, B. (1995). Learning style preferences of physical education majors: Implications for teaching and learning. *Journal on Excellence in College Teaching, 6*(2), 57–77.

Randall, L. E., & DeCastro-Ambrosetti, D. (2009). Analysis of student responses to participation in literature circles in a university classroom. *Journal on Excellence in College Teaching, 20*(2), 69–103.

Rea, L. M., & Parker, R.A. (2005). *Designing and conducting survey research: A comprehensive guide*. San Francisco: Jossey-Bass.

Richlin, L. (2001). Scholarly teaching and the scholarship of teaching. *New Directions in Teaching and Learning, 86*, 57–68. San Francisco: Jossey Bass

Riggs, E. G., Gholar, C. R., & Gholar, C. R. (2009). *Strategies that promote student engagement: Unleashing the desire to learn*. Thousand Oaks, CA: Corwin.

Robinson, J. M., & Nelson, C. E. (2003). Institutionalizing and diversifying a vision of the scholarship of teaching and learning. *Journal on Excellence in College Teaching, 14*(2/3), 95–118.

Rodgers, C. (2002). Defining reflection: Another look at John Dewey and reflective thinking. *Teachers College Record, 104*(4), 842–866.

Salkind, N. J. (2006). *Exploring research* (6th ed.). Upper Saddle River, NJ: Pearson.

Salkind, N. J. (2009). *Exploring research* (7th ed.). Upper Saddle River, NJ: Pearson Prentice Hall.

Saunders, M. D. (1998). The service learner as researcher: A case study. *Journal on Excellence in College Teaching, 9*(2), 55–67.

Saunders, G., & Klemming, F. (2003). Integrating technology into a traditional learning environment: Reasons for and risks of success. *Active Learning in Higher Education, 4*(1), 74–86.

Savory, P., Burnett, A. M., & Goodburn, A. (2007). *Inquiry into the college classroom: A journey toward scholarly teaching*. Boston, MA: Anker.

Saylor, C., & Harper, V. (2003). The scholarship of teaching and learning: A faculty development project. *Journal on Excellence in College Teaching, 14*(2/3), 149–160.

Schon, D. A. (1983). *The reflective practitioner*. New York: Basic Books.

Schon, D. A. (1990). *Educating the reflective practitioner: Toward a new design for teaching and learning in the professions*. San Francisco, CA: Jossey-Bass.

Shapiro, H. N. (2006). Promotion & tenure & the scholarship of teaching & learning. *Change* (March/April), 39–43.

Shulman, L. S. (2004). Visions of the possible: Models for campus support of the scholarship of teaching and learning. In W. E. Becker & M. L. Andrews (Eds.), *The scholarship of teaching and learning in higher education: Contributions of research universities*. Bloomington, IN: Indiana University Press.

Shulman, L. S. (2011). The scholarship of teaching and learning: A personal account and reflection. *International Journal for the Scholarship of Teaching and Learning, 5*(1). Retrieved May 10, 2011, from http://www.georgiasouthern.edu/ijsotl

Simon, H. A., & Kaplan, C. A. (1989). Foundations of cognitive science. In M. I. Posner (Ed.), *Foundations of cognitive science*. Cambridge, MA: MIT Press.

Solomon, D. J. (2001). Conducting web-based surveys. *Practical Assessment, Research & Evaluation, 7*(19), Retrieved May 11, 2010, from http://PAREonline.net/getvn.asp?v=7&n=19

Sperling, C. (2003). How community colleges understand the scholarship of teaching and learning. *Community College Journal of Research & Practice, 27*(7), 593–601.

Spezzini, S. (2010). Effects of visual analogies on learner outcomes: Bridging from the known to the unknown. *International Journal for the Scholarship of Teaching and Learning, 4*(2).

Stefani, L. (2011). Current perspectives on SoTL. *International Journal for the Scholarship of Teaching and Learning, 5*(1). Retrieved May 10, 2011, from http://www.georgiasouthern.edu/ijsotl

Stewart, D. W., & Shamdasani, P. N. (1990) *Focus groups: Theory and practice*. Thousand Oaks, CA: Sage.

Taylor-Powell, E., & Renner, M. (2003). *Analyzing qualitative data*. Retrieved May 18, 2010, from http://learningstore.uwex.edu/assets/pdfs/G3658–12.pdf

Teddlie, C., & Tashakkori, A. (2009). Foundations of mixed methods research: Integrating quantitative and qualitative approaches in the social and behavioral sciences. Los Angeles, CA: Sage.

Teve, R. (2006). *Qualitative data analysis*. Retrieved May 18, 2010, from http://earticles.info/e/a/title/qualitative-data-analysis/

Tinberg, H., Duffy, D. K., & Mino, J. (2007). The scholarship of teaching and learning at the two-year college: Promise and peril. *Change, 39*(4), 26–33.

Tollefson, K., & Osborn, M. K. (2008). *Cultivating the learner-centered classroom: From theory to practice.* Thousand Oaks, CA: Corwin.

Treisman, P. U. (1990). Studying students studying calculus: A look at the lives of minority mathematics students in college. *College Mathematics Journal, 23*, 362–372.

Trigwell, K., & Shale, S. (2004). Student learning and the scholarship of university teaching. *Studies in Higher Education, 29*(4), 523–536.

Tsang, A. (2010). Pitfalls to avoid in establishing a SoTL academic pathway: An early career perspective. *International Journal of the Scholarship of Teaching and Learning, 4*(2), 1–9.

Visioli, S., Lodi, G., Carrassi, A., & Zannini, L. (2009). The role of observational research in improving faculty lecturing skills: A qualitative study in an Italian dental school. *Medical Teacher, 31*, (8), 362–369.

Weckman, J., & Scudder-Davis R. (2005). Teaching natural science to nonmajors: A comparison of two different course formats—The "team of experts" vs. the "individual instructor." *Journal of Excellence in College Teaching, 16*(1), 149–169.

Weimer, M. (2002). *Learner-centered teaching: Five key changes to practice.* Jossey-Bass Higher and Adult Education Series. San Francisco, CA: Jossey-Bass.

Weimer, M. (2006). *Enhancing scholarly work on teaching and learning: Professional literature that makes a difference.* San Francisco, CA: Jossey-Bass.

Weimer, M. (2008). Positioning scholarly work on teaching and learning. *International Journal for the Scholarship of Teaching and Learning, 2*(1), 1–6.

Weiss, R. S. (1994). *Learning from strangers—The art and method of qualitative interview studies.* New York: The Free Press.

Werder, C., & Otis, M. (Eds.) (2009). *Engaging student voices in the study of teaching and learning.* Sterling, VA: Stylus.

Willig, C. (2008). *Introducing qualitative research in psychology.* Berkshire, UK: McGraw Hill.

Willis, J. (2006). *Research-based strategies to ignite student learning: Insights from a neurologist and classroom teacher.* Alexandria, VA: Association for Supervision and Curriculum Development.

Witman, P. D., & Richlin, L. (2007). The status of the scholarship of teaching and learning in the disciplines. *International Journal for the Scholarship of Teaching and Learning, 1*(1), 1–17.

Wong, F. K. Y., Kember, D., Chung, L. Y. F., & Yan, L. (2005). Assessing the level of student reflection from reflective journals. *Journal of Advanced Nursing, 22*, 48–57.

Woodhouse, R. (2010). Hype of hope: Can the scholarship of teaching and learning fulfill its promise? *International Journal for the Scholarship of Teaching and Learning, 4*(1), 1–8.

WSU's Critical and Integrative Thinking Rubric. Retrieved May 18, 2010, from https://my.wsu.edu/portal/page?_pageid=177,276578&_dad=portal&_schema=PORTAL

Wyandotte, A. (2009). Reciprocal gains in higher order thinking and course content in teaching students to argue and think critically. *Journal on Excellence in College Teaching, 20*(4), 31–53.

Yin, R. K. (2008). *Case study research: Design and methods.* Newbury Park, CA: Sage.

Index

Also available from Stylus

Exploring Signature Pedagogies
Approaches to Teaching Disciplinary Habits of Mind
Edited by Regan A. R. Gurung, Nancy L. Chick, and Aeron Haynie
Foreword by Anthony A. Ciccone

"*Exploring Signature Pedagogies* is a remarkable achievement that is sure to find its way onto everyone's short shelf of essential books on teaching and learning. Here we see more evidence that the scholarship of teaching and learning can no longer be described as an 'emergent' field, but is well into its prime and yielding some of the most exciting and potentially transformative discoveries in higher education today. The ambition of the project is breathtaking: to give fourteen Cook's tours of selected disciplines across the arts and sciences, highlighting each field's distinctive habits of head, hand, and heart and how these habits form—or more often, fail to inform—how teaching and learning is done with undergraduates. But the real contribution of the volume lies in the authors' recommendations for how disciplinary fields might develop signature pedagogies that enact and perform the disciplines' core concerns. This linking of teaching practices to the specific disciplines being taught makes the concept of signature pedagogies an improvement on older pedagogical enthusiasms such as active learning. It also fully demonstrates the claim that teaching, when properly conceived, is exciting intellectual work. Thus, this is the perfect book to give to faculty members who are dubious of 'faddish' education research. It also belongs in the hands of every beginning teacher or anyone wanting a good road map to the problems and possibilities of teaching the liberal arts. Departments will want to discuss the chapters devoted to their discipline, while SoTL researchers will find the collection useful for imagining the next generation of research. In short, there is something here for everyone, making *Exploring Signature Pedagogies* one of the best portals of entry to the scholarly literature on teaching and learning in higher education."—***Lendol Calder***, *Associate Professor of History at Augustana College, currently represents the Organization of American Historians on the board of the National Council on History Education.*

Exploring More Signature Pedagogies
Approaches to Teaching Disciplinary Habits of Mind
Edited by Nancy L. Chick , Aeron Haynie , and Regan A. R. Gurung
Foreword by Anthony A. Ciccone

"Essays exploring the signature pedagogy in a discipline provide a systematic account of the relation among evidence, methodology and the teaching of the field. This second volume of essays greatly expands the menu of fields of study presented in this engaging and generative way. While there is enormous benefit to us all from reading deeply in educational research literature, most faculty members find it more compelling to consider powerful ideas and tools in education when they are situated within familiar topics, challenges, and intellectual goals. Progressive teaching now takes an inductive approach, starting from students' existing experience, interests, and understanding and moving toward general understanding of phenomena and conceptual synthesis of intellectual work. In the same way, this volume continues the effective articulation of characteristic teaching within specific fields of study, making it more likely that professors from many fields will meaningfully engage the literature of education research in general."—***Dan Bernstein***, *Director, Center for Teaching Excellence, and Professor of Psychology , University of Kansas*

Engaging Student Voices in the Study of Teaching and Learning
Edited by Carmen Werder and Megan M. Otis
Foreword by Pat Hutchings and Mary Taylor Huber

"*Engaging Student Voices in the Study of Teaching and Learning* illustrates the pedagogical power of extending the teaching and learning relationship to form an engaged and interactive partnership inside and outside the classroom. Not only does this book ground the practices of engaging students in developing and implementing the learning process theoretically, it illustrates the successes and challenges of establishing a shared responsibility for conceptualizing and constructing knowledge and ways of knowing. A must read for those teachers seeking to increase student engagement and to enhance each student's self-authorship in the learning process."—***Barbara Mae Gayle***, *Academic Vice President , Viterbo University*

This book addresses the all-important dimensions of collaboration in the study of learning raised by such questions as: Should teachers engage students directly in discussions and inquiry about learning? To what extent? What is gained by the collaboration? Does it improve learning, and what do shared responsibilities mean for classroom dynamics, and beyond?

22883 Quicksilver Drive
Sterling, VA 20166-2102

Subscribe to our e-mail alerts: www.Styluspub.com